Live More, Spend Less

Visit our How To website at www.howto.co.uk

At www.howto.co.uk you can engage in conversation with our authors – all of whom have 'been there and done that' in their specialist fields. You can get access to special offers and additional content but most importantly you will be able to engage with, and become a part of, a wide and growing community of people just like yourself.

At www.howto.co.uk you'll be able to talk and share tips with people who have similar interests and are facing similar challenges in their lives. People who, just like you, have the desire to change their lives for the better – be it through moving to a new country, starting a new business, growing their own vegetables, or writing a novel.

At www.howto.co.uk you'll find the support and encouragement you need to help make your aspirations a reality.

You can go direct to **www.live-more-spend-less.co.uk** which is part of the main How To site.

How To Books strives to present authentic, inspiring, practical information in their books. Now, when you buy a title from How To Books, you get even more than just words on a page.

Live More, Spend Less

A Savvy guide to saving money for all the family

SARAH FLOWER

SPRING HILL

For my wonderful husb
To the world, you are o
to me you are the worlc

London Borough of Barnet	
Askews	Oct-2009
332.024	£9.99

Published by Spring Hill, an imprint of How To Books Ltd.
Spring Hill House, Spring Hill Road
Begbroke, Oxford OX5 1RX United Kingdom
Tel: (01865) 375794
Fax: (01865) 379162
info@howtobooks.co.uk
www.howtobooks.co.uk

British Library Cataloguing in Publication Data
A catalogue record of this book is available from the British Library

ISBN: 978 1 905862 34 4

Produced for How To Books by Deer Park Productions, Tavistock, Devon
Designed and typeset by Mousemat Design Ltd
Printed and bound by Bell & Bain Ltd, Glasgow

NOTE: The material contained in this book is set out in good faith for general guidance and no liability can be accepted for loss or expense incurred as a result of relying in particular circumstances on statements made in the book. Laws and regulations are complex and liable to change, and readers should check the current position with relevant authorities before making personal arrangements.

Contents

Acknowledgments	viii
Foreword by Janey Lee Grace	ix
Introduction	xiii
1 Money Matters	**1**
The Boredom Trap	3
Keeping Up with the Jones	4
The Emotional Spender	5
Getting the Buzz	5
Kids' Pressure	6
Financial Contacts	7
2 The Home	**8**
Utility Bills	9
Gas and Electricity – Top Tips to Lower Bills	9
Heating Your Home	20
Cutting Water Bills	23
Home Telephone and Broadband	26
Mobile Phones	29
Buying and Selling Property in a Recession	32
Improve, Don't Move	35
3 Cleaning the Home	**38**
Store Cupboard Essentials	42
Everyday Cleaning Tips	46
Trouble-shooting	53
The Scented Home	56

4 Food and Drink — **61**
Getting the Right Equipment — 63
Putting your House in Order — 66
Great Food Ideas — 68
Look After Your Fruit and Vegetables — 71
Money Saving Tips for Grocery Shopping — 73
The Good Life — 80

5 Recipes — **85**
The Basics — 88
Meat — 94
Fish — 98
Vegetarian — 100
Soups — 104
Baking — 108

6 Beauty — **115**
Main Factors for Good Skin — 117
Make-up Savvy — 118
Professional Pampering — 121
Natural Skincare and Beauty — 125

7 Clothing — **136**
Budget Clothing — 137
Designer for Less — 142
Vintage Style — 143
Love the Skin You're In — 144
You're Hired — 145

8 Raising the Family — **146**
The Formative Years — 147

Watch Them Grow	154
Teenage Angst	163
9 Transport	**168**
Cars	169
Rail	177
Flying	179
10 Holidays	**180**
Holiday Swaps	181
Working Holidays	183
Hobby Holidays	184
Hostels	184
Camping and Caravanning	184
Budget Holiday Deals	185
Eco Holidays	187
11 Make Do and Mend	**188**
Repair, Reduce, Reuse, Recycle	189
Make Your Own Gifts	193
12 Earning Extra Money	**196**
I Could Do That...	198
Keep Start-up Costs Low	200
Retraining	202
You're Hired!	202
Money for Old Rope	204
Cash-back Sites	206
Index	**207**

Acknowledgements

A huge thanks to my fantastic husband Terry, who has encouraged and supported me in everything I have done since we first met. The endless cups of tea, constant reassurance and supplies of chocolate have made this happen – though it has not helped my waistline!

To my gorgeous boys, I am so proud of you both. Orri, you have taken the art of money saving to a different level – more hippy tightwad than savvy thinker, but love your style. Tamlin, my beautiful boy – I fear we have a long way to go on the money saving front. Only five years old and already a complete shopaholic and your penchant for drama and ladies' handbags has me in stitches.

Mum and Dad, for years you despaired, wondering what would become of a child whose only skills were storytelling, cooking and being a bossy boots. Years later, these skills have given me the career I love. Thanks for the Sunday cooking marathons, the sewing lessons I hated and for teaching me to create my own opportunities in life.

Thanks to Janey Lee Grace for her support. To Nikki and the team at How To Books. Thanks for believing in me enough to make this book a reality. Finally, thanks to Jennifer McEwan from *My Weekly* for supporting this project.

Foreword

I am delighted to be asked to write a foreword and a section on frugal but fun ways to bring up babies and toddlers for this excellent book. For many years, I've been passionate about holistic living, writing books and running a website and forum with the sole aim of encouraging everyone to take responsibility for their own health and wellbeing and to look after the planet in the process. I must confess though, mine is not altogether an altruistic striving; the reality is I'm determined to be healthy and happy but I'm also very thrifty by nature. The current economic climate notwithstanding, I have always loved seeking out bargains and looking for a 'make do and mend' solution before shelling out any hard-earned cash. I came from a fairly poor background but I'm extremely grateful that it taught me to be savvy when it comes to budgeting and to nurture an uncanny knack for finding absolute treasures in other people's cast-offs and second-hand goods.

To this day, irrespective of how much money I have, I have always opted for charity shop chic. Why wear exactly the same kit as everyone else when you can create your own unique look with a mixture of retro, last season, designers' samples and funky accessories for the price of a pizza? Of course, it's now seen as being responsible to recycle everything including clothing and accessories so I consider myself rather smugly ahead of the game.

To this end I love Sarah's book – what a wonderful collection of tips and ideas, some tried and tested that we just needed to be reminded of, such as holding clothes swap parties (and I love her suggestion of checking what size friends are when you invite them to attend so that there's swappable items for everyone) through to really informative information on the best rates for utility bills and how to reduce your energy use in the home.

It's lovely to be reminded of old-style common sense. We know that in wartime people were healthier, they ate less, they ate seasonally and organically because they mostly grew their own food and had none of the expensive pesticides we have today.

If you'd suggested 'recycling' to a wartime housewife, she would have thought that meant getting back on her bike when she fell off, and yet they recycled automatically: socks were darned, leftovers were made into many more meals and bathwater (after the whole family had bathed in it) was re-used to flush the toilet or clean the yard.

Sarah's book reminds us to make use of what we have and improve our homes rather than look to move. She offers excellent quick recipes not only for cheap, nutritious family meals but also for simple 'do it yourself' skincare and cleaning solutions. (I'm looking forward to trying the fabulous recipe for homemade furniture polish.)

The really great news is that by putting into place many of the ideas in this book you will not only save money, you'll also be healthier and you can tick the eco box almost without trying. By re-using, mending, making your own and generally going a bit old style, you will automatically reduce your carbon footprint without needing to compromise. There is also something extremely therapeutic about saving money and being sustainable and, without doubt, in the currency of contentment you'll be rich indeed.

Janey Lee Grace
Author of *Imperfectly Natural Woman*
and www.imperfectlynatural.com

Introduction

I have always loved a bargain. I like nothing better than scrambling around at boot sales, junk shops and antique fairs and I am positively euphoric when I sell or win a bargain on eBay. However, I am a bit of a snob. I want only nice things around me but I will seek out the best bargain before I commit. I think nothing of spending a couple of hours researching the best price for my fridge, or hours losing the will to live in order to shave a few pounds off my car insurance. I will not however walk around in rags, living off boiled cabbage and baked beans in order to have a healthy bank balance. Life is too short. Woe betide anyone who tries to drag me away from my computer or tell me that I should not have the latest BlackBerry Storm. I want the best of both worlds: to save money, enjoy life and buy the occasional must-have gadget.

I believe that we can give our children the best childhoods and save money. We don't have to stigmatise them by living like a pauper. Sending them to school clutching mung bean salads and driving them around in a clapped-out Volvo overflowing with recycled rubbish is really not for me.

This book is a guide for households to dip in and out of, as and when they require. It is not a guide to go without, but a guide to inspire and ultimately to give you a life while saving money. I don't like using the term frugal or thrifty – both words conjure images of living a grey life, dressed in old tat and becoming obsessed about reusing your teabags. I actually knew a lady who did just that. She also washed and reused cling-film. If it works for you, then fine, but sorry, I won't be including these gems in this guide. If you are looking for a guide on how to live on 20p a day, this is not for you, so walk away now. If, however, you are looking for ways to cut down on your spending but maintain the same standard of life, what are you waiting for? Get reading now!

I was brought up in the 1970s in a small village in Devon. My parents struggled financially but managed to give us a wonderful childhood. We lived within a council estate – albeit another world from how we would imagine inner city estates. We had manicured lawns, a great community spirit and social and moral values enforced by the entire village – a bit like living with one big extended family. Everyone knew each other and their personal business. No computers, games consoles or children's TV. We enjoyed playing games, running around in the fresh air and using our imaginations.

I was very lucky. Compared to children nowadays, my life was relatively straightforward. We were able to be children and had much more freedom to play than kids today. The community spirit ensured we were being watched over. We were safe and happy. I have two children and, even though I live in a sleepy Devon village, I cannot let them roam as free as I did. I don't think the world is a nastier place – there were as many perverts and child molesters in the 1970s as there are today I am sure. The main difference is lack of community. We don't look out for each other any more. We are blind to everything around us apart from our own little lives. I find that very sad. As parents, we now have to create our children's entertainment. With busy lives, that inevitably means relying on TV, computers and games consoles, as our children become increasingly isolated from the great outdoors.

My childhood followed a strict moral code. Adults were respected – whether they were your parents or your next-door neighbour, you did as you were told. Things weren't handed to you on a plate; you had to earn them. Personally, I think this makes the resulting enjoyment far greater. We want something, we get it; five minutes later, we want something else … and so it goes on. My five year old is a nightmare to take shopping. He does not understand that he can't have what he wants when he wants it. Things are given too easily. I am guilty. I have resorted to bribery on many occasions – 'Be good and you can have x', or whatever is needed to calm troubled waters. My parents would never have done that. It would have been 'Be good or you will get a clip across the ear'. Gifts were only given to me on birthdays, Easter, holidays and Christmas, and yet I never went without.

I was taught the practical side of life. On Sundays, my mum and I would bake cakes, biscuits and pies for our packed lunches during the week, while preparing our Sunday roast. I learnt to sew, knit and clean the house. I enjoyed it; it made me feel grown up and was great bonding with my mum.

I have tried to make this guide practical for real life. We don't all have time to make our own butter or even in some cases grow our own vegetables. To me money saving is not just about the pennies, it is also important to include your time. Spending three hours making your own jam, to find you only have enough to fill two jars, is not really that economical. The main point I am trying to make in this book is to be a savvy thinker.

Dip in and out of the pages and use this as a reference to help point you in the right direction. Some tips are simply common sense but, as is life, it takes someone to point them out before we realise what is right in front of our nose.

Good luck and happy saving!

CHAPTER ONE

Money Matters

'A BANK IS A PLACE
THAT WILL LEND YOU MONEY
IF YOU CAN PROVE
THAT YOU DON'T NEED IT'
Bob Hope

1

Money Matters

This book is about money saving on a daily basis. I am not a financial expert so I am not going to include any legal, financial or banking advice. There are many financial organisations, books and websites to help if you are having financial difficulties and I have included some useful contacts at the end of this chapter.

I would advise anyone concerned about money to make a budget. If you find this difficult, you can download a great budget tool from www.moneysavingexpert.com Do not lie in this budget; you are only lying to yourself. Be as honest as possible and include everything. If you are not sure of amounts, look at your bank statements, credit card statements or even start a diary to highlight where and why you are spending. You cannot start making changes until you have identified where you are spending your money.

Our relationship with money is quite a complex one. We buy for many reasons, the least of which is necessity. Take away your everyday household expenses (mortgage, insurance, utility and food) and you are left with the non-essentials. What do you buy and why? Do you need it? Will you use it? Can you afford it? Can you buy it cheaper elsewhere? It is all too easy to listen to the little shopaholic devil sitting on your shoulder, urging you to spend, spend, spend. I am certainly not telling you never to buy anything nice again, just to know what you are doing and the real reason why.

The Boredom Trap

Six years ago, I was lucky enough to fulfil a lifelong ambition and own my own horse. We lived in a farm cottage so we were able to have horses on our doorstep for no extra outlay. Our horses lived out all year round, were hardy and needed little maintenance. Taking away the expense of the horses, I noticed a difference in our lifestyle and spending. Weekends were no longer spent walking around our nearest town, lunching and buying treats. Suddenly I was too busy to want or need to do this.

Looking through bank statements, we realised we were saving over £300 a month. We had not cut back. We ate the same, we had the same bills; all that had changed was not going out spending due to boredom.

Sadly, we had to move several years later and could no longer keep our horses. Once again, we noticed a change in spending patterns. Weekends, especially in the colder months, were spent in and around shopping centres. We were bored so we used to spend. We would create excitement by convincing ourselves we needed to buy a new car, a TV or whatever it was that would give us the temporary buzz. Once we had purchased that must-have item, we would move swiftly on to the next need. I have spent hours in computer shops, convincing myself to update my perfectly usable computer for a better, faster model. Once home, I then spend more hours setting it up to be exactly like the old one I have discarded.

EBay is a great example of passion buying. You can spend hours and hours looking at items, and with a painless click, you can purchase. I have spent many lovely hours bidding on clothing. Just small amounts ... a fiver here, £3 there. Before I know it, I have spent over £80 including postage. It is only when the garments finally arrive that I discover some don't fit or are not what I was expecting. I know a friend who purchased a jukebox one night when he had had too much to drink. It is too easy to spend and to satisfy that burning itch to have the next best thing.

Keeping Up with the Jones

This is a very real issue. How many of us have bought items we could not really afford to keep up the image? Maybe a friend or colleague has something and you want to go one step better? Have you acquired a new friend and you want to be just like them? We all do this; it is human nature. The key is to identify that you are doing this. Little do you know, but the friend or colleague could be up to their eyes in debt – do you really want to emulate that? We all know people who have lost money. That posh new car, the gorgeous house, the designer clothes – all mean nothing when the debts start mounting up. Happiness is something no one can take away from you. Start to find areas in your life that really make you happy and content. Surround yourself with friends who allow you to be yourself.

The Emotional Spender

We have all been there. Feeling blue, down in the dumps and life is just so unfair – why not go to the shops and buy something to make you feel better? Yes this can work wonders (until you get the credit card bill), but there are other ways to feel good. Feeling emotional, lonely, upset or heartbroken is not good for shopping. A bit like walking into a supermarket when you are very hungry – you will suddenly find you have a trolley full of snacks but no substance. The clothing lurking in the back of your wardrobe, unworn and unloved, was probably bought on a day when you weren't yourself – how else do you explain those purple flares? Much better and cheaper to stay at home, watch a good film and eat a ton of chocolate.

Getting the Buzz

There is nothing like the buzz or adrenaline rush spending can give you. Whether it is a new car, designer outfit or holiday – it is a great feeling. However, it can be very short lived. Find the buzz a different way. I love the feeling of finding a bargain – knowing I have something I want for a great price is fantastic.

My home is Victorian and filled with period-style furniture and an eclectic mix of objects – all junk shop or boot sale finds. We are always getting compliments on our furniture or the way we have put things together. Yet we have probably not spent more than £30 on any one item.

If I need a new appliance, I can spend hours searching the internet for the best product for my needs and the best price. If you only have a small budget for clothes, why not investigate second-hand clothing retailers or buy discounted designer finds online? For the same price as a new high street item, you could have a designer or vintage piece that will turn heads. It is all about savvy thinking. Why pay more when you don't have to? The buzz is from knowing you have saved money yet still got what you were looking for.

Kids' Pressure

Children are exposed to buying pressure every day. Watch children's TV and the adverts will put huge pressure on the child to have the latest toy or gadget. Once at school, the need to be accepted by their peers extends to having the right clothing, toys and gadgets. It can be increasingly hard for parents to stand up to this demand.

Every Christmas families get deeper into debt, often just to give their children the best Christmas they possibly can. We all know Christmas is on the same day every year, so why don't you budget for it? Same with birthdays: budget, budget, budget. It is also vital to teach your children from a young age the value of money. There is no shame in living within your means. Show them the fun things in life. Do you recall the presents and toys you had as a child, or do you remember the fun days out, the friendships, the great outdoors? Spend time with your children. See Chapter 8 on 'Raising the Family' for more ideas.

Whatever your reason to spend, identify it for what it really is. Only then can you start to change your spending habits.

The Citizens Advice Bureau

For information and help on a wide range of issues including debt, contact your local Citizens Advice Bureau or visit www.citizensadvice.org.uk

National Debt Helpline

For free independent advice on debt, call the national debt helpline on 0808 808 400 or visit www.nationaldebtline.co.uk

Debt Divas

I like this site – real women helping others with financial problems. Go to www.debtdivas.co.uk

Are you claiming the right benefits?

Need to know what benefits or help you may be entitled to? Families can claim family working tax credits, child benefits and may be eligible for help with council tax and their rent. Pensioners may not be receiving their full benefits. To check if you are able to get help, visit a great website called www.entitledto.co.uk You can then contact your local Social Security office or visit www.direct.gov.uk for more information.

CHAPTER TWO

The Home

'WE NEED NOT POWER OR SPLENDOUR,
WIDE HALL OR LOFTY DOME; THE GOOD,
THE TRUE, THE TENDER, THESE FORM
THE WEALTH OF HOME.'
Sarah J. Hale

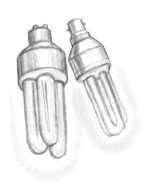

Our homes eat money. We have to maintain them, clean them, heat them, furnish them and entertain in them. They are our biggest investment and often our biggest worry. According to statistics released by Direct Line Insurance, British households spend £217 billion a year running their homes. When I add up how much it costs to live in our home, I can start to see the appeal of buying a motorhome and taking to the open road.

This chapter covers all aspects of money saving in the home. Whether you are worried about increasing utility bills or looking for a money-saving gadget, this chapter should help.

Utility Bills

Electricity, mains gas and oil central heating help make our lives so much better, but the increasing rise in costs are causing many of us a great headache. With some savvy thinking, you can lower you bills.

Gas and Electricity – Top Tips to Lower Bills

Become a monitor
You can now buy electricity monitors for as little as £30. A word of warning – you will get a little paranoid at first! Watching the monitor reading accelerate every time you use your kettle will give you a great incentive not to

overfill it. You can buy monitors from electrical stores or online. I like the OWL wireless electricity monitor – £34 from John Lewis, but to be honest they all do pretty much the same thing.

First Utility is the first energy supplier to offer a smart meter. The smart meter allows customers to see what, when and where they are using their energy. This information is fed back to First Utility every 30 minutes to ensure accurate bill readings, and, with three daily tariffs, consumers can choose tariffs that suit their energy consumption.

Don't under estimate

It is important to inform the supplier of the units you have used. Estimates are not a good idea. Don't fall into a false sense of security by under estimating in order to cut your monthly costs. It will catch up with you in the end! Get into the habit of giving your supplier an accurate reading regularly to ensure you are only paying for what you used.

Make yourself heard

If you are having problems paying your utility bills, speak to the company concerned. Don't bury your head in the sand and hope it will go away. It won't. They may suggest a different tariff or, if you have a backlog of outstanding bills, a prepay meter may be offered. Prepay meters are charged at a higher rate, but there are plans to get this lowered. No matter how stressed you are, avoid getting angry with your supplier. If you are nice and polite, you are more likely to get help.

Get yourself on the right tariff

Are you on the right tariff for you? Speak to your provider to consider the options available to you. You may find Economy 7 or Economy 10 will suit if you use most of your electricity at night. Other options are dual energy tariffs, which are great if you get your electricity and gas from the same supplier. You could make an estimated saving of up to £400 a year just by opting for an online tariff, with added discounts for online paperless billing and direct debits. You could opt for fixed price tariffs – though be careful you don't set yourself at a price when other companies are lowering their prices.

Spread the cost

If you struggle to pay your quarterly bill, speak to your supplier about monthly payments. One suggestion is to estimate your usage during the winter months and continuing paying this rate throughout the summer. By the time the following winter comes around, you will be in credit.

To switch or not to switch

Switching to a cheaper supplier has never been easier. Use comparison sites such as www.uswitch.com, www.energyhelpline.com or visit www.switchwithwhich.co.uk to find the best deal in your area. However, a word of warning: there is a right time and a wrong time to switch. If you are unsure, I would strongly recommend visiting www.moneysavingexpert.com as this website will highlight when it's the best time to switch. At the time of writing, the utility companies are all reducing their prices, so until this is settled it would be foolish for anyone to switch provider. If you are looking for a green energy provider, have a look at www.greenenergyswitch.com

Turn down the heat

Without leaving you cold, why not turn your thermostat down a few degrees. You will save money without really noticing. Turning down your thermostat by just 1 °C could save you £30 per year.

Wrap up

We all moan about our heating bills, but I have many friends and family who like to have the heating on and to walk around their homes in thin t-shirts. By wearing more layers of clothing, you can save pounds on unnecessary heating costs.

Using the same principle, wrap up your home. If you are on benefits or aged over 60, you may be eligible for an energy efficiency grant. Contact the Energy Saving Trust on 0800 512 012 or visit www.est.org.uk

Install insulation, especially in the loft, around immersion heater and cavity walls. You can save an estimated £200 a year. Visit www.thinkinsulation.com for more tips and advice.

Placing heat reflectors behind radiators will throw heat back into your room, giving an estimated 25% more heat.

If you don't have double-glazing, why not opt for secondary double-glazing. An inexpensive company is www.365plastics.com with prices starting from as little as £40 a window with no DIY necessary as they attach using magnetic strips. I live in a Victorian house overlooking the Atlantic. Our home is a listed building with old sash windows, so replacing them was not an option. We used 365plastics and the difference is amazing. Fitting was very simple, with no drilling or DIY required.

Carpets insulate better than hard flooring. Statistics show that having your rooms carpeted can reduce your annual heating bill by at least £60 a year.

Make the most of your radiators and heaters. Make sure they are not obscured by furniture or covered by furnishings. Never put clothing or items on your radiators to dry.

Crafty draughty

You have insulated and wrapped up your home but you may still have some problem draught areas. Consider the following ideas:

- Install thick door curtains and heavy curtains in main rooms to keep heat in. It also helps if you close the curtains at dusk.
- Fit draught excluders around doors and windows.
- One of the biggest problem areas is unused fireplaces. The chimney balloon costs £19.99 and is a simple yet clever device. Simply inflate the balloon to block the chimney cavity. Unlike the cheaper alternative of stuffing the chimney with newspaper, the chimney balloon will shrivel and deflate if accidently heated. The device is available from www.chimney-balloon.co.uk
- Close doors to keep heat in the rooms. If there is still a draught, why not make a draught excluding sausage dog out of scraps of fabric.
- If you have sash windows that rattle and can't afford

to replace them, you could opt for the secondary double-glazing option described above. If you can't afford these changes, you can revert to the traditional draught excluding techniques. Place newspaper in the gaps of the sash windows and carefully seal the edges with masking tape (as this can be easily taken off in the summer months).

Paint that keeps you warm

Really, I am not going mad. Insulating paint additive, ThermilateTM, is a powder that makes paint insulate! According to www.thegogreencompany.com the microspheres within the powder act as mini thermos flasks. ThermilateTM powder is mixed with ordinary paint (one pack mixes into five litres of paint) to make an insulating coating that can keep heat in or out. It is ideal for insulating buildings, rooms, water tanks and even hot or cold water pipes. Priced at only £19.95, I think this is well worth the money.

Say goodbye to your old boiler

If your boiler is over ten years old, you are probably wasting a huge amount of energy. According to Northern Gas Heating Company, around 60% of CO_2 emissions from your home are down to your boiler. With an efficient new boiler, you could save up to 875 kg of CO_2 and £130 a year, and a new condensing boiler could cut gas bills by nearly 40% or £150 per year for a typical semi-detached house. Add in a full set of heating controls as well as a new boiler, and you could increase the total savings to around £250 and 1.7 tonnes of CO_2 per year.

Stand up to standby

Standby uses a shocking amount of electricity. Get used to turning things off at the mains. Leaving items on standby can cost the following:

- DVD player: from £1 – £4.50 per year
- DVD recorder: from £2 – £14 per year
- Freeview box: from £3.50 – £15.50 per year
- Computer monitor: from £30 per year
- Printer: from £15 per year
- Microwave: from £7 per year
- Cooker: from £7 per year
- Cordless phone: from £8 per year
- Stereo: from £10 per year
- Widescreen plasma TVs use more electricity than a fridge-freezer
- PC, printer, scanner, router and speakers cost £240.90 a year to power if on every day, according to www.Efergy.com

If, like me, you have your DVD, sky box, and TV on one extension lead – why not opt for a device that automatically turns them all off. I use the One for All Energy Saver universal remote control, which costs £34.99 from electrical outlets. With an estimated saving of up to 90%, it will pay for itself in no time.

Similar devices are available for computers (such as the Eco Button at £14.99). These work by activating your computer's energy-saving 'sleep' mode, saving oodles of watts in the process, and it comes with clever software that carefully records the energy and money you have saved.

Light up your life

We spend 10% of our energy bills on lighting. We should all have the message now about the importance of energy efficient light bulbs. Swapping traditional light bulbs for energy efficient bulbs can save £10 per bulb per year. At the time of writing, Asda are offering four energy bulbs for £1 so it really does pay to switch.

Other ideas for saving on lighting costs include:

- Get in to the habit of turning lights off when leaving a room.
- Remove net curtains and clean windows and skylights to make the most of the natural light.
- Use timer switches or sensor switches to keep lighting to a minimum.
- Paint your walls with bright, light-reflecting colours.
- Clever use of mirrors will help lighten dark areas of a room or hallway.
- Candles create a relaxing and intimate atmosphere – and, if scented, can help keep your home smelling sweet.

The big freeze

Fridges and freezers use up a shocking amount of electricity. If you need to replace your fridge or freezer, make sure you opt for the most energy efficient: A-grade fridges will save you approximately £35 a year.

To help your fridge or freezer run more efficiently, try the following:

- Replace your plug with gadgets such as the SavaPlug to help reduce electricity consumption by up to 20%.
- Defrost your fridge and freezer regularly.

- Keep your fridge and freezer at least three quarters full. If you have a large chest freezer and cannot fill it with food, place cardboard boxes or rolled up newspaper to help fill it up.
- Do not leave the fridge or freezer door open longer than necessary.
- Make sure the door seals are working correctly.
- Do not place warm or hot food into the fridge or freezer – allow the food to cool first.
- Keep air circulating around the fridge or freezer, particularly around the condenser coils at the back. Clear the condensers of dust regularly as dust can reduce efficiency by up to 25%.

Washing day

Washing machines all have energy efficient cycles and this can cut the cost of your electricity bill. In a recent survey by *Which?* magazine and website (www.which.co.uk), Ariel Excel Gel was voted best buy at 30°C, tackling stains such as chocolate ice cream and even bolognaise sauce with ease. This gel works out at 22p a wash which, although is more expensive than other brands, should save you money by cutting down your electricity costs. *Which?* also reviewed washing liquids at 40°C, and surprisingly Sainsbury's basic biological came top of the list and, at only 9p a wash, it is a real bargain.

Tumble dryers are expensive and should really only be used in emergencies. Get into the habit of letting nature dry your clothes – nothing beats the smell of freshly washed clothes dried on the washing line. If this is not practical, why not get an indoor drying rack. I use a wooden, Victorian-style laundry maid, which allows me to hang my clothes then hoist out of the way. Heat rises and my clothes are dry within a few hours.

A clean plate
Dishwashers can save time, money and water if used correctly:
- Make sure you always have a full load before turning it on.
- Use the most energy efficient setting.
- Help the dishwasher out by clearing the plates of food scraps before loading.
- Keep the filters clean.
- Once a month, put on a cycle when empty to keep the filters and pipes clean.

In a review of dishwasher tablets by *Which?*, Finish Powerball Max came top for combination tablets but, at 24p a wash, it is not the cheapest option. Tesco Value, which are detergent only tablets (so you must add salt and rinse aid), came top at only 6p a wash, with Lidl W5 coming a close second. For those who want a green detergent, try Ecover at 19p a wash.

The great British cuppa
We all enjoy our cuppa, but kettles use a huge amount of electricity. Buy the most energy efficient kettle you can. Kenwood has a great eco kettle, which reduces consumption by up to 35%, or you could opt for the one-cup machines (Tefal and Breville offer these). They use the same amount of electricity as a standard kettle but for a

much shorter period – 6 seconds per cup as opposed to 2 minutes in a kettle. I tried both these but if, like me, you prefer to make a pot of tea and use the kettle to boil water for cooking, you will be better with the traditional style Kenwood Eco Kettle. If you are lucky enough to have an Aga or Rayburn, why not keep a kettle on the stove. To help reduce your energy consumption, make sure you only boil the water you need and de-scale your kettle regularly.

Be on the boil

Never heat a pan of water from cold. If you need hot water for cooking, use the kettle to heat it, not the stovetop. This will save time and energy.

Cook with savvy

Make use of your oven. I have some great memories of my mum and I spending our Sunday mornings baking whilst also preparing the Sunday roast. We would bake cakes, pies and pastries to last us the whole week, making the most of the oven space. This principle has stayed with me. Whenever I use my oven, I always make sure I fill the shelves well and utilise the heat.

There are some great gadgets on the market to help save on oven costs. I love the JML Halogen Oven at £59.99 in which I have prepared a roast, jacket potatoes and even a fruitcake. It cuts electricity costs and reduces cooking time. Jackets were done in less than an hour and still maintained that oven-cooked crispness. It saves putting on the oven for only small items.

You can also get combination microwaves. LG

SolarCube, priced at £159, combines an oven, microwave and grill. Other models are available from £75.

Buy wisely

When you need to replace your old appliance, remember to buy the most energy efficient model available. Look at the star rating for more information. It may cost you a few pounds more but think of the long-term savings. *Which?* is a great source of information and reviews, and offers a 30-day free trial – great for some investigation time.

Heating Your Home

During the winter months, we need to do all we can to keep our homes warm and snug. Following the advice given above for gas and electricity savings can help ensure a warmer home. *Which?* has reviewed the most popular heating sources for homes. The following prices are shown for winter 2008/09 and do not include installation costs.

Type of Heating		Price per Annum
Gas heating and hot water	Condenser boiler	£490
	Standard boiler	£730
Electric heating and hot water	Economy 7/10 tariff	£870
LPG heating and hot water		£830
Oil heating and hot water	Condenser boiler	£740
	Standard boiler	£1100
Wood heating and hot water		£510

Whatever heating system you use, make sure you have it regularly serviced. If you need to replace your boiler, opt for a condenser boiler.

Oil central heating

Oil central heating is the choice of many households, particularly those in rural areas. There was a huge hike in oil prices in 2008 – almost double the cost from the previous year. Thankfully, the price is starting to come back down but it is still expensive. Ways to lower costs include the following:

- To make sure you have the best price for your area, log on to www.boilerjuice.com Simply type in your postcode and it will show the cheapest price.
- Share the order. If your neighbour orders oil, why not combine orders to get further discount from your supplier.
- As with gas and electricity, lower your thermostat to help reduce your heating costs.
- Make sure your boiler is serviced regularly. If you buy a new boiler, opt for a condenser boiler to lower costs.

As oil prices have risen, there has been a rise in oil theft. Make sure your oil tank is locked and protected from opportunists. It is a good idea to shield your tank from view.

Wood and coal

Wood is making a bit of a comeback. Many of my friends have wood burners or solid fuel stoves. If you are lucky enough to have access and permission to collect dead wood and fallen trees, you can keep your fires burning all winter long. If you opt for delivery, buy your wood from a reputable dealer. Seasoned logs are best. Never buy your wood in small bags from a service station – you will be paying through the nose!

Mixing coal and wood together can help give the fire body and make the fuel last longer. We put coal on the fire at night and cover with a sprinkle of ash or potato peelings. The fire keeps in all night.

You can make your own logs using old newspapers. I have done this and, although it's good fun, it can get very messy. To make the logs, you have to soak the paper, then place in a log-maker, clamp and press out the excess water. It is a messy process. Place the wet logs somewhere to dry – I normally make them in the summer months and leave them outside in the sunshine to dry. You will need to store the wet logs until they are dry enough to stack. Newspapers are best for making logs, but I have been successful adding handfuls of shredded paper. You can add wood chips, twigs, dried leaves and even dried teabags. My dad used to add coal dust to his bricks.

Wood ash is great for the garden and can be used in a variety of ways. However, if you burn coal, you will have to think of other alternatives to dispose of the ash. Coal ash can be used on pathways as it kills the weeds and, if you have some clinker or lumps of coal remaining in the ash, it can bind to form a good base for a pathway. As with all ash, make sure it is cold before you dispose of it.

Cutting Water Bills

Water prices are increasing. Your water bill is estimated on the rateable value of your home – so the bigger your home, the larger your water bill, even if you live alone. If you have a big house and only a few people who live in it, it may be worth getting a water meter fitted. You can do a quick check online by logging on to www.uswitch.com

Whether you have a water meter or you want to do your bit for the environment, you will want to take measures to keep your water consumption to a minimum. The following table shows typical water consumption in the home.

Bath (filling the tub)	80 litres
Dishwasher (one cycle)	40–50 litres
Toilet (one flush)	6–9 litres
Shower (five minutes)	30–40 litres
Power shower (five minutes)	80–90 litres
Washing machine (one cycle)	50–60 litres
Hose pipe (per minute)	500 litres

Save water – shower with a friend

Remember the slogan? Now there is another way to cut the quantity of water used in your shower – simply change your showerhead. Companies making products such as Awatea Satinjet and EcoCamel showerheads estimate that you can save over 40% by opting for a showerhead that reduces water consumption. An average shower uses 40 litres; switching to a more energy efficient showerhead can reduce this by half, without affecting the quality of your shower.

Tap into it

For as little as £5, you can buy a tap aerator. These aerators have integrated flow regulators that reduce the rate of your water flow by as much as 60% – for example, from 15 to 6 litres per minute.

Visit www.biggreensmile.com for more information.

Plug it in

Whether you are washing up, washing your face or cleaning vegetables, remember to pop the plug in to conserve water. This can save approximately 5 litres of water.

Tooth waste

You can lose up to 10 litres of water every time you brush your teeth if you leave the tap running. Use a mug of water to rinse instead.

Flush proof

Flushing the toilet can use up to 9 litres of water. Some people advocate only flushing when you do a number two ... I personally couldn't do this as I don't like the smell of stagnant urine in my toilet and, with four of us in the house, it could get quite fruity!

Another less odorous solution to save water is to install a device into your cistern such as the Save-a-Flush or Hippo the Water Saver. Some water companies offer these free of charge. If buying a new toilet, why not opt for the most energy efficient. Most new cisterns have a dual flush. For those who want to opt for the green option, you can choose a composting toilet. For more information visit www.compostingtoilet.org

Here's one I prepared earlier

Running the tap until it is cold enough to drink, wastes water. Why not fill a jug and pop it into the fridge providing chilled water whenever you need it without waste. We all need to drink more water and filling a jug is a great way to monitor your water intake.

The cuppa

As mentioned above, don't overfill your kettle. Using only the water you need saves water and electricity.

Machine savvy

Dishwashers and washing machines do save money and water if used correctly. Make sure you always have a full load and use the most energy efficient settings. See the above section on electricity saving for more information.

Rainwater collections and harvesting

B&Q estimates that 85,000 litres of rainwater fall on your home every year. There are great devices on the market to help you harvest and conserve this water. A water butt is essential for those who need to water their garden. You can also fit a great device to utilise the water from your guttering and even your (non-soapy) bath water. If you have the room and budget, why not opt for a complete rain harvesting system to use in your home and garden. For more information visit www.rainwater-harvesting.co.uk

Gardeners can make the most of their water by following the following tips:

• Use water butts to collect rainwater. If you have a

large garden, have more than one water butt or, if money permits, opt for a complete rainwater harvesting system.

- Cover your water butt to protect it from contaminants and to prevent evaporation.
- Use a watering can instead of a hose to save water.
- Use a mulch to cover the soil in your flowerbeds, helping to keep the moisture in the soil and preventing weeds.
- Hanging baskets and tubs need regular watering in the summer months. Mix the compost with water-retaining crystals to help keep the soil moist.
- Never water in direct sunlight. You will scorch the plants and you will waste water through evaporation.

Home Telephone and Broadband

Finding the right telephone provider for you can be a bit of a minefield. Add the need for broadband packages and even TV subscription offers and you really can give yourself a headache. According to comparison sites, I am currently with a more expensive provider. I have been lazy and kept with my usual provider for both telephone and broadband. I am happy with the service but I know I may have been able to save a few more pounds a month if I had looked around.

According to telecoms regulator Ofcom, there were almost 17 million broadband connections in the UK by the end of September 2008, with the number rising every year. I would be lost without an internet connection. It is my personal gateway to information, money saving and the outside world. The big debate is the cost of the packages. Do you combine your telephone and broadband package, or do you shop around for individual packages?

A lot depends on your personal circumstances, telephone and broadband usage and whether or not you are in an existing contract (as there could be penalties incurred if you break away early). I can't tell you which provider will save you the most money – this changes on an almost daily basis. However, just as with mobiles, you need to make a list of what you require from your provider. This could be free telephone calls in evenings and weekends, or it may suit you more to have free landline calls 24/7. Your broadband usage may be low or, if you are like me, you use it all the time. Whatever your preference, there should be a package to suit you.

If you are stuck in a contract and don't want to incur penalties, you can have an overrider provider. By dialling a code before every call, you transfer your call package to another provider. The website www.moneysavingexpert.com has details of the best deals on offer, or you can use a comparison site such as www.uswitch.com

Don't pay to call 0870

Phoning 0870, 0871, 0844 and 0845 numbers is becoming increasingly expensive. For BT customers, you can now dial 0870 and 0845 numbers without charge as part of your free call package. If you are not with BT, you may have to spend some time doing a bit of investigating. Often companies will list a landline number especially for those calling from overseas. You may be able to find the landline number of a company through internet searches or by using directory enquiries online. Failing that, there is a great website www.saynoto0870.com where you can search for alternative numbers for your chosen company.

Don't pay to call directory enquiries

Most directory enquiries services cost money, with high price per minute plus a standard connection rate. If you use the internet, use free online search services such as BT's phone book, Thomson Local, 192.com and Yell.com If you are unable to access the internet, you have limited choice. 0800 100 100 is a free directory enquiries service but it can often be busy. Others such as the Number (0800 118 3733) is free to use but may involve annoying advertising.

Phoning from mobiles will cost substantially more. DQ4Mobile offers a simple text service. Text '83211' to search and retrieve telephone numbers from a national directory of over 1.5 million businesses. Calls cost 25p per text. However, if you can access the internet via your mobile, then this probably is the cheapest option for you.

Calling overseas

Skype is the perfect way to stay in touch and chat to a loved one anywhere in the world free through high quality voice and video calls as well as instant messaging. With 405 million registered users worldwide, there is a big chance that some of your friends and family are already users, so if you call each other using Skype, your calls would be free.

Alternatively, you could 'speak' online through one of the messaging services – MSN is very popular and immediate. You can even transfer folders, which is great if you want to share photos or documents. You can buy a webcam for under £10 if you want to see each other.

Don't leave children unattended when they are using the internet. Be vigilant if they are using social networking sites and chat rooms. When using a webcam, make sure it is positioned in a living area, not a bedroom as this has been known to help prevent abuse.

Mobile Phones

Can you remember a time when we relied on phone boxes and home phones? Nowadays we start to panic if we can't contact someone immediately. Mobile phones have become an essential part of our existence. The good news is that deals are getting better. The key is to know how you will use your phone. If your phone is for emergencies and the odd call or text, you would be better off with a pay as you go option. Maybe you text more than you call, or you need email or Blackberry service. Once you know what you want to use your phone for and how often you use it, you will then be able to find the best deal for you.

Some pay as you go options offer free evening and weekend calls or free texts per month. Contracts no longer have to be long-term. O_2 offer 30-day contracts starting at £10. Orange was the first to offer a pay as you go Blackberry.

Shop around before you commit yourself, and don't

forget to look online for the best offers. Comparison sites can save you a huge amount of legwork so use them. As always, the best are www.moneysupermarket.com, www.onecompare.com and www.uswitch.com

Don't fall for pretty packages

I am the world's worst for falling for a shiny new gadget. Give me a new techno toy and I will be a very happy bunny. Be very careful when choosing a tariff or contract based on the package offered. One example was the 'free' notebook with mobile broadband contracts offered in 2008/09 by some companies. Everyone rushed out to get their freebie. Sadly, it was all smoke and mirrors. The tariff was more than that offered by other providers, but this was ignored in favour of the free laptop. If you calculated the cost of the additional tariff charges over the period of the contract, they amounted to more than the laptop was actually worth. Suddenly the package looks less appealing.

Don't get stuck in a rut

Mobile phone companies change their tariffs and deals frequently. Don't get stuck in a rut and stick with the same deal. This applies to pay as you go as well as contracts. My husband was with O_2 on their monthly contract: 300 minutes plus 200 texts for £15 a month, and unlimited calls to all O_2 numbers. A great deal. While checking his online bill, we noticed O_2 were offering a monthly contract for £10 for slightly less minutes and texts. This package suited him better than the £15 so we seamlessly switched, saving £5 a month.

Communication saves money

Get into the habit of speaking to your provider on a regular basis just to check you are getting the best deal for you. If you find a better deal elsewhere but don't want to change providers, there is no reason why you can't call and ask them to match the deal. More often than not, they will do this rather than risk losing you as a customer.

This works well with most utility services, not just mobile phones. My mum signed with Orange broadband. She did not want to go through the hassle of changing providers and risking losing service for a short time, but she was annoyed that other providers offered significantly cheaper rates. I persuaded her to let me speak to them to see if we could reduce the bill. After a painful 20-minute call, I got her three months free broadband and a reduction of the ongoing bill by almost half. It certainly pays to talk. Remember the rules: always be polite, courteous and smile (yes, smiling on the telephone really does make a difference – you can almost hear the smile!) and never ever lose your temper.

Recycle your old mobile

There are some great sites on the net where you can earn money from your old mobile phone. Before you commit, check out a few sites as prices do vary. When I upgraded to my new Blackberry, I wanted to sell my old one. EBay would have been the best option but I had lost the box and instruction booklet and I did not fancy any hassle from disgruntled buyers. I looked online and found the pay-back price varied from £30 to £75 – quite a difference. If you are feeling altruistic, you could always donate yours to a charity.

Try these sites for cashback deals for your old mobile:
- www.envirofone.com
- www.moneysupermarket.love2recycle.com
- www.mopay.co.uk
- www.mobilephoneexchange.co.uk
- www.mazumamobile.com
- www.bananagreen.com

Buying and Selling Property in a Recession

Buying and selling a property, which often represents the largest financial commitment in people's lives, is stressful at the best of times. However, in a recession the anxiety can be triplefold.

So when property prices are falling by 25%, houses and flats are on the market unsold for over a year and no one has any money, how do you go about buying or selling a property quickly to ensure that you get the results you want? Mark Brogan from Express Estate Agency (www.ExpressEstateAgency.co.uk) has some great tips to help if you are buying or selling. They deal with people facing these issues every day, and can help to sell or buy quickly. They are currently selling ten times more properties a week than the national average.

Securing finance – The property market has changed beyond recognition. With mortgages now effectively rationed, it's essential to know how to obtain the best mortgage deal and to understand the way credit scoring and credit systems work. A good independent mortgage broker should be able to help.

Choosing a reputable mortgage lender and surveyor can mean the difference between success and failure in selling or buying a property quickly. We recommend to all our sellers that they have a Royal Institution of Chartered Surveyors valuation of their property and then reduce the cost of this by a minimum of 10% before putting it on our website. Often this results in multiple block viewings and then bids for the property, which have led, in some cases, to the property selling at the original valuation price.

Information gathering – From April 2009, every home put on the market must have a Home Information Pack (HIP). This brings together valuable information at the start of the process – such as a sale statement, local searches and evidence of title – which saves the purchaser money, time and stress but can add pressure for the seller. The Pack also includes an Energy Performance Certificate (EPC) that contains advice on how to cut CO_2 emissions and fuel bills.

HIPs provide key information needed by buyers and sellers at the very start of the home-buying process, making transactions more efficient and less likely to fall through between offer and exchange.

If you put in the hours… If you want to sell or buy a property quickly, take control of the procedure and dedicate time to finding the right mortgage and legal advice. Use the internet to check property prices in your area. Be ready to proceed quickly with finance in place and solicitors available, that way both buyers and sellers avoid many of the traditional hurdles that can slow down the process, such as onward chains collapsing, something that is increasingly common in the current property market.

Save money by appointing a reputable, progressive estate agent that has a 'No Sale, No Estate Agency Fee' policy plus no exit fees, and is a member of the Ombudsman for Estate Agents. An excellent online presence with trained advisers and negotiators available 24 hours a day, seven days a week is also preferable, as you never know when you might need that little bit of extra advice!

Get your property ready to market

You can improve the desirability of your property by spending some time getting it ready for sale. Try to view your property with fresh eyes. Does the entrance to the property look clean and desirable? Is the interior too cluttered to see the full potential? Are the colours too vibrant to attract a new buyer? Spending time and money to prepare your property for market can greatly increase your chances of a sale. Neutralise the interior colours, declutter, clear the gardens and make your home welcoming. If you are unsure, look at some show homes and see how they are presented.

Smells are also important. If you smoke, have animals or eat a lot of fried food, you home is going to have lingering smells which might put potential buyers off.

Think about this before taking viewings. Wash dog beds, throw out the fryer and smoke outside for a day or so before a viewing. Fresh coffee, home-baked bread, open fires, fresh flowers and scented candles all help to create a welcoming atmosphere.

Improve, Don't Move

With house prices plunging, savvy homeowners are now choosing to improve, rather than move. The practice of 'interior styling', rather than 'interior design', is fast becoming a popular service, with good reason. Interior stylists specialise in re-inventing your space to create a fresh, designed look without breaking the bank. This is achieved by re-arranging your existing belongings, sourcing bargain furniture and accessories, plus secret styling tricks. Zoe Brewer, creative director of My Interior Stylist Ltd, has kindly passed on a few of her clever tips for creating a beautiful home. Minimal cash required.

De-clutter and organise. Most homes have hoards of unused items, in varying proportions. Clearing these and organising storage makes a marked difference to your home (and mind) and is a great place to start on a home makeover. Set aside a day just to concentrate on the clear out.

Clear your wardrobes – if you haven't worn something for two years, it should go.

Paperwork is another big offender. To deal with articles you are keeping for reference and any other necessary information, scan as much as possible into your computer and file on a hard drive (and back up). Put out all old newspapers, magazines and paperwork for recycling, shredding anything with your personal details included.

For everything else, have four bags on the go: eBay, charity, Freecycle and rubbish. Organise everything you need to keep in appropriate, well-labelled storage. Don't be afraid to get rid of things you don't like just because they were a present or are valuable. Selling them will give you some extra cash to buy something you like for your home. Charity shops are struggling at the moment, so will appreciate anything that they can sell.

Furniture placement. How a room is arranged will affect how people use it and the general vibe. Moving a sofa can feel like a whole new room! To help with ideas, draw a plan of your room, and cut out paper shapes, to scale, for your main furniture. Then you can play around with different options, without having to lift heavy items repeatedly. Try to find a focal point in the room, for example a fireplace, and work around that. Contrary to popular belief, arranging seating against the wall, around the edge of a room, does not make the room seem bigger.

Revamp your colour scheme. A new colour scheme can be added to a room relatively quickly and cheaply. Look at your main items of furniture and consider the colours you have to work with. Pick an accent colour that will coordinate with this. You can look through interior design magazines for ideas. Create a feature wall by choose one wall to paint or wallpaper in a different shade to the rest of your walls. Pick up this colour throughout the room with cushions, throws, candles, flowers, and so on. These items can be sourced from supermarkets, high street shops and markets.

Create your own art. Art is a personal thing, and people often want to wait until they come across something they love. In the meantime walls remain very bare and cold. Having things on the wall completes a room, so why not make your own. Buy some canvases and get creative. This is a great way to use up tester pots of emulsion. Children come in handy here too for a bit of abstract work!

Another idea is to buy lots of different frames in different styles, and spray them all the same colour. Use them to frame your favourite photos (black and white prints look best) and arrange to create one large 'masterpiece'. Why not take some precious or sentimental items and display them in a box frame. This way you get to appreciate them every day, rather than having them stored away out of sight.

Clean, clean, clean. Finally, have a good old clean, including all those areas that normally get missed – under beds, top shelves, and so on. Clean windows with lemon juice and newspaper to allow maximum light into your home.

All of the above are quick, easy and relatively cheap ideas to make the most of your home. If you would like to know more about interior styling and Zoe's services, visit www.myinteriorstylist.com

CHAPTER THREE

Cleaning the Home

'CLEANLINESS AND ORDER ARE NOT MATTERS
OF INSTINCT; THEY ARE MATTERS OF
EDUCATION, AND LIKE MOST GREAT THINGS,
YOU MUST CULTIVATE A TASTE FOR THEM.'
Benjamin Disraeli

Keeping our homes clean and fresh can seem like a never-ending and often thankless task.

The spring-cleaning research carried out by Vileda (www.vileda.co.uk) revealed:

- 52% of Brits spend less time cleaning than their parents did.
- An amazing one-fifth of Brits have never been shown how to clean properly, not knowing the difference between their sponges and their scourers!
- We have never been more time pressured – Brits admit to not having the time to spring clean their homes.
- While we aren't cleaning enough, a staggering 98% admit to feeling much happier when they have a clutter-free home.

We have become a society with very little practical home skills. Cooking, cleaning, and DIY are alien concepts to many. We are looking for the magic product that can clean our home without any effort from us. Manufacturers have picked up on this, hence the aisle upon aisle of products in supermarkets to help clean our home with minimum effort … but maximum expense. Some products are good, some bad and some totally unnecessary. If you want your house looking good but don't want to put any effort in – employ a cleaner, otherwise you will have to use a bit of elbow grease and get stuck in.

A recent survey claims households in the UK spent over £100 million per year on cleaning products, with each household spending an average of £33.64 per month. I am not immune to the buying frenzy. I have strange bottles lurking under my sink – some have been there for years. I am the first person to try the latest miracle-cleaning product on the market and, yet, I always end up sticking to my old favourites. If we look back over the years, our ancestors used very little to clean their homes, relying more on elbow grease and products found in their store cupboards than costly manufactured cleaners.

In the past century or so, cleaning and hygiene have played a major role in improving our health and both the length and the quality of our lives. Keeping our clothes, our environment and ourselves clean – without spending a fortune – is not merely a luxury but a necessity.

There is much confusion about the wide choice of cleaning products available today and many believe that you can either be 'green' or pay less – and that the two are incompatible. However, by rethinking your cleaning habits the truth is that it won't cost the earth (in either sense). In fact, being 'thrifty' often goes hand in hand with being green. I have invited the cleaning experts, the UK Cleaning Products Industry Association, to explain.

The term 'natural' means lots of different things to different people and an enthusiasm for all things 'natural' is a defining trend of our time. Yet the common expectation that 'natural' products will inevitably tend to be 'safer' is not supported by fact. Some of the most dangerous substances known to humans are found in plants after all – to take just one example, rhubarb leaves contain oxalic acid that can cause kidney problems or convulsions and induce coma.

It is important to demystify the facts about 'natural' ingredients versus 'chemicals' used in washing and cleaning products. This is not just because belief, which is not based on sound science, is misleading but also because where myths abound you could be persuaded to spend your money needlessly on products whose supposed 'natural' superiority isn't quite what it seems.

Instinctively many people seem to feel that substances can be subdivided into those that are 'natural' and those that are not. Yet all 'things' are composed of the same 90-odd chemical elements that exist in the world and from which everything is made. Therefore the separation of things 'natural' from things that are 'chemical' is irrelevant and essentially meaningless.

If you are keen to save money you might just find that one of the best ways to do so is to be green whilst you clean. You may need to rethink your choices. If like most of us you thought that doing your bit for the environment ended at the checkout, you'll need to think again.

Take laundry for instance. With regard to energy use, our choice of laundry product is, according to the experts, only 20% of the process; the big impact, the remaining 80%, is how you choose to use the product. Washing a full load and not a partial load and selecting a lower temperature for your wash will save money and help the planet. The same is true when it comes to how much of a product you use. Choosing the correct dosage each time will also have a positive effect and it is easy to do – just follow the instructions on the pack.

Further reading

The UK Cleaning Products Industry Association has published a discussion paper, *Meeting Natural Expectations*, which is available to download from www.ukcpi.org or, if you prefer a printed copy, email ukcpi@ukcpi.org

Below, I highlight cleaning tips using store cupboard products. You will be surprised at the results. They not only save you money, but they may be better for your health and the environment. If I have not done enough to convince you and you're still yearning for your branded goods, why not try downshifting to supermarket-own brands.

Store Cupboard Essentials

We have gels and liquids, washing up liquid and sprays, surface cleaners of all descriptions, hob cleaners, oven cleaners, sink unblockers, polishers for various surfaces, wipes, floor cleaners – and on and on the list goes. Are they all necessary? Analyse your cleaning routine in the kitchen and identify the products you use on a regular basis. You will probably be surprised at the result. Combine your favourite can't-do-without products with some store cupboard recipes, and you will save money and have great solutions to everyday cleaning problems.

We all have our favourite must-have products. I use a combination of brand and store cupboard cleaning, whilst using natural scented candles to create a welcoming aroma and atmosphere. (Beware, there are some nasty, cheap, scented candles on the market that not only smell horrible but can also be dangerous to your health.)

Bicarbonate of soda

This is a wonderful must-have product. It is cheap and safe and has a wide range of uses from cleaning, stain removing, unblocking and even odour eliminating. Don't buy it from the cake section in your supermarket – it will cost you so much more. Buy in bulk. I buy from a local discount store, but you can also buy online in large 5–6 kg packages from www.summernaturals.co.uk

White (distilled) vinegar

White vinegar is cheap and safe, used for cleaning, de-scaling, odour eliminating and stain removal. The strong smell from using vinegar will disappear once dry.

Lemons

Lemons are fresh smelling and naturally acidic, so they work well as a cleaning ingredient. They have antibacterial properties and can act as a natural disinfectant and bleach.

Salt

You may already know about pouring salt onto wine stains, but salt has many other great uses within the home and, like all of the above, it is cheap and natural.

- Mix salt with turpentine to form a paste. Use this on yellowed enamel such as bathroom sinks and toilets to help restore and clean them. Use coarse sea salt to make a wonderful exfoliator for your skin (see Chapter 6 on Beauty).

- Add salt to cold water to help remove fresh blood stains from fabrics.
- Pour salt straight onto burnt pans and leave for 15 minutes before scrubbing.
- Soak a washed dog bed in a salted water solution before drying as this helps to repel fleas.

Tea tree oil

This is an absolute essential in our home. I use it as part of my cleaning regime and because of its antiseptic, antifungal, antiviral and antibacterial properties, it can be used for a number of health and hygiene problems.

- Wash hair with tea tree shampoo to help repel head lice. It can also help to eliminate dandruff.
- Due to its antibacterial and antiviral properties, it is an excellent disinfectant.
- Add to your washing machine to help disinfect and freshen – great for pet bedding!

Lavender oil

Lavender is a great calmer and has antiseptic properties so it is ideal to use around the home.

- It is wonderful to have lavender oil burning when someone has a cold. Its antibacterial properties could help prevent germs spreading, and its calming properties are perfect for those needing to rest.
- Place a few drops on the temples to help calm headaches.
- Add a few drops to a cotton cloth and place in the tumble dryer with bedding to create a lovely calming and relaxing scent.

• Make a room spray by adding lavender drops to water and use this as an air freshener and relaxing bedtime spray.

Value baby wipes

If you like the convenience of wipes, swap your branded, purpose kitchen and surface wipes for value baby wipes. Baby wipes are also great for wiping down stainless steel, dusting and for cleaning leather upholstery.

Value brand washing powder

I use liquid washing detergent in my washing machine, however I like to keep some value washing powder in my cupboard for a multitude of cleaning jobs.

Linseed oil

Linseed oil is a fantastic wood preserver. It also helps to add moisture to the wood and can give back its rich, vibrant colour. I use it periodically on all wooden surfaces, particularly floorboards and doors. Add lavender oil or your favourite essential oil to create a lovely smell. Olive oil can also be used as a polish, but add some great smelling essential oils to create the right aroma.

Bleach

Not natural I know, but I do resort to this for particular jobs around the home. For those who like more environmentally friendly products, Ecover offer a bleach powder. You can add the powder to water to make liquid bleach for use around the home or use the powder for whitening laundry.

Value denture tablets

Great for removing stains and, if you buy the value range, they will be relatively cheap to buy.

Tools of the trade

- Hard and soft bristle brush and dustpan sets
- Old toothbrushes
- E-Cloths and Clever Cloths by JML are both great value for money, all-purpose cloths that help trap the dirt and clean more effectively than standard cloths, even without additional cleaning products
- Newspaper
- Value aluminium foil

Everyday Cleaning Tips

Oven cleaner

If you have ever used the brand chemical cleaners, you will know how uncomfortable and often toxic cleaning the oven can be. As an alternative, try using a paste made up of bicarbonate of soda and water, which you can use to coat the dirty areas of a cold oven. If areas are particularly stubborn, leave overnight before wiping away.

If you're fed up with cleaning your grill or oven, why not place a sheet of aluminium foil in the grill pan or base of the oven to catch any spills. Cleaning is then simple – just remove the sheet and replace.

Hob cleaner

For stubborn areas, use equal parts of salt and bicarbonate

of soda. Sprinkle over the hob and leave for up to 30 minutes before rinsing off. You can use non-scratch scourers if particularly stubborn, or keep hold of your old toothbrushes for some hard to reach areas.

For stainless steel hobs, finish with a polish using a baby wipe.

Disinfectants

We are obsessed with disinfecting our homes. You can make your own disinfectant by adding 3 tbsp of borax with 1 litre of hot water and 10–15 drops of tea tree oil.

Surface cleaner

- Half fill a spray container with hot water. Add 10 drops of tea tree or lavender oil, 3 tbsp of white vinegar and 2 tsp of bicarbonate of soda and shake thoroughly.
- Mix equal measures of washing powder with salt and bicarbonate of soda to tackle tough stains.
- Keep surfaces stain free by using chopping boards and heat resistant mats.
- Keep a saucer or small pot near your hob on which you can place mixing spoons while cooking.
- For very stubborn stains such as tea, curry, pasta sauce and red wine, make your own spray bleach. Fill a spray container with water and add a small amount of bleach or Ecover bleach powder. Label the container so you know which one contains the bleach.

Dishwasher and washing up

- As with any machinery, a dishwasher works more

effectively if it is looked after. If you are using all-in-one dishwasher tablets, you do not need rinse-aid or salt. Always read the label to ensure you are using the products correctly.

- Sprinkle washing powder onto greasy pans and oven dishes to help dissolve the grime. Leave stubborn stains to soak overnight.
- Metal scourers are expensive. To make your own, simply scrunch up a ball of aluminium foil.
- Always scrape the plates before loading the dishwasher to avoid food waste blocking the filters.
- Rinse all dishes and pans that are covered in oil, gravy or pasta sauces to avoid stains, particularly if using the eco-wash cycle.
- Add one cup of white vinegar to an empty hot wash to help prevent the build up of limescale and to help keep the dishwasher fresh and clean.
- Place half a lemon in the cutlery tray to freshen.

Fridge

To keep your fridge fresh and clean, following these simple steps:

- Place a small pot of bicarbonate of soda in the back of the fridge to absorb unwanted odours.
- Half a lemon is great to keep the fridge smelling fresh.
- Wash shelves regularly with your own blend of surface cleaner (see instructions above).
- Regularly clear out your fridge from unwanted items and food that has gone off – though by following the food and drink tips in Chapter 4, you will keep this kind of waste to a minimum!

- I line the trays with old t-towels to help absorb moisture. This also avoids nasty smells accumulating.

Drains

- Never put oil, tea or coffee grains, food or vegetable peelings down the drain, as this will cause a blockage.
- Invest in a metal plug filter for less than £1 (available from hardware stores) to prevent food waste escaping down the plughole.
- To deal with blockages, pour one cup of bicarbonate of soda down the plughole followed by one cup of white vinegar. Leave to fizz for 30 minutes.

Bins

- Rubbish bins need to be emptied regularly to avoid nasty smells.
- It is false economy to use cheap, thin dustbin bags – you often end up having to double them up and cope with the fall-out from split bags. I always buy biodegradable bags but ensure they are thick enough to avoid splitting under weight.
- Save money on expensive bin fresheners. Simply sprinkle value washing powder in the bottom of dustbins to keep fresh.
- Put 'smelly' food straight into your outside bin to avoid creating smells within your home.

Toilet

There is nothing more offensive than a dirty toilet. Supermarkets are bulging at the seams with sprays, liquids and gels to create a clean and fresh smelling toilet, but nothing really beats hard work and savvy.

- Toilet brushes are unhygienic. I liked the Toilet Duck Brush, but the refills are expensive, so instead of using the refills I gather a bundle of toilet paper and clip on the end of the brush. It works just as well and there's no mess and no waste.
- Half fill an empty spray container with water, 3 tbsp of bicarbonate of soda, 10–15 drops of tea tree oil and 4 tbsp of white vinegar and shake well. Use this as a toilet spray. Leave for 20 minutes before cleaning with a toilet brush (see alternative above).
- I find the smell of some toilet fresheners almost as offensive as a dirty toilet. I have a selection of perfumes I have picked up from boot sales for next to nothing, which are great to use as room fragrance. If we have visitors arriving, I will put some scented candles around the house and one in the bathroom.
- Value denture tablets and even value cola can be used as substitute toilet cleaners.

Windows and mirrors

My husband has always cleaned windows using vinegar and scrunched up newspaper. Mix up a solution of half water and half vinegar and spray onto the window or mirror. Wipe away with scrunched up newspaper for the perfect finish.

Mirrors steaming up in the bathroom seem to be a particular bugbear for many. I have found many tips and all seem to work with varying degrees of success. Small amounts of shaving foam, washing-up liquid, hair conditioner and even toothpaste rubbed into the mirror and wiped off thoroughly all claim to prevent a build up of steam.

Bath and sink
• To avoid soap build up, why not opt for a liquid soap. It can save mess and is more hygienic.
• Get your taps gleaming – soak some kitchen towel or toilet paper in lemon juice and wrap it around the taps. Leave for an hour and rinse.

Shower
• Showerheads can often get clogged with limescale. Mix a solution of half water and half vinegar, and submerge the showerhead in it for a minimum of 20 minutes to help dissolve the limescale. Rinse thoroughly before using.
• To prevent shower curtains from getting mildew, allow the curtain to dry before you push it to one side.
• Clean glass shower doors with the window cleaning solution (half water, half vinegar) and wipe with scrunched up newspaper.

Mildew
• Mildew can look unsightly. To prevent the build up, make sure the bathroom is well ventilated. Open the bathroom window to let air circulate on a daily basis.
• For existing mildew, use a bleach solution. This helps kill any spores and stops the area from getting any worse.
• For discoloured grout, try scrubbing with an old toothbrush and whitening toothpaste.

Curtains and blinds

Keep curtains and blinds clean and dust free. Curtains benefit from being washed at least twice a year.

Carpets

Having wooden flooring in some of my rooms has made me realise how much dust and grime must accumulate in the carpets. I have a very good vacuum cleaner but the floors still benefit from sweeping around the edges of the rooms, and particularly down the staircase, with a stiff brush.

Wood and laminate

- Sweep regularly – especially in the corners where you will find a frightening amount of dust accumulating.
- Keep wooden floors in tiptop condition by waxing or oiling.
- Don't use harsh cleaners on your laminate flooring.
- To remove scuffmarks from laminate, try using a normal pencil eraser.

Homemade furniture paste

This is a recipe found in a notebook of my neighbours used during WW2:

> 3 oz beeswax
> 1 oz white wax (candle ends)
> 25g curd soap (white Winner)
> 500ml boiled water
> 500ml turpentine
> 30 drops of lavender essential oil (I have added this to the recipe as I can't resist the smell!)

Boil the water. Shred the soap and wax into the water. Heat gently until all has melted. Add the turpentine and essential oil, stirring all the time until cold. Bottle for use.

Trouble-shooting

Clothing stains

Before using any of the following natural remedies on fabrics, I advise doing a spot test to make sure the fabrics will not stain or bleach. Avoid using these techniques on delicate fabrics.

- Blood – If you have blood on clothing or fabric, soak immediately in cold water to remove the worst of the stain. Soak tough stains in a solution of water, vinegar and bicarbonate of soda. For mattresses, mix a thick paste of bleach and talc. Once dry, you can brush off – don't use this on upholstery as the bleach will stain the fabric.
- Everyday clothing stains – There are many stain-removing remedies. Choose what works for you.
  - ‣ White vinegar applied neat to a tough stain.
  - ‣ White vinegar and bicarbonate of soda solution sprayed onto the stain before placing into the washing machine.
  - ‣ Ecover laundry bleach or a whitening formula added to washing detergent to help with white washes.
- Grease stains – These can be removed by making a paste of bicarbonate of soda with cream of tartar (2 to

1), mixed with a little water. Apply to the stain and leave to absorb before adding to your wash.
- Vomit – Soak in a strong solution of bicarbonate of soda and water before adding to your wash.
- Perspiration marks – These can be removed by spraying with a strong vinegar solution before adding to the wash.

Wall marks

Bread is as effective as the branded 'magic' erasers now on the market. Scrunch into a ball and rub over offending marks. For crayon marks, toothpaste is effective. For everyday grubbiness, try value baby wipes.

Hair dye

Dying your hair can be a messy business. I put a carrier bag over my hair to prevent mess while waiting for the formula to set, and I always use an old towel. Try to mop up spills as quickly as possible. Bath sealants and grout can often get tarnished with dye. To remove this you can use thick bleach or try whitening toothpaste.

Red wine

Red wine is supposed to be easy to remove if you pour lots of salt onto the spill. I have never been that successful so in this case I would recommend a branded product. Wine Away is used by Loire Valley wine-tasting school. Apparently, they always have some on hand for their wine-tasting courses, so it comes highly endorsed! It can be used on fabrics, upholstery and carpets, and a little goes a long way!

Spilt milk

Spilt milk can leave a rather unpleasant stagnant smell if it's not removed completely. One tip is to pour a combination of bicarbonate of soda with talc over the spill and leave for 24 hours. Vacuum when dry.

Removing stickers/labels

I hate sticky labels, especially the ones you try to peel off gently but end up with a horrible mess. Gently dab the label with olive oil or even WD40. Leave for a couple of minutes and then it will simply peel away like magic!

Tea-stained mugs

Dishwashers are good at getting rid of tea stains, but if you are still suffering, there are some simple solutions:
- Spray the inside of the cup with a bleach solution (or Ecover Bleach) and leave for a few minutes before washing and rinsing thoroughly.
- Soak stained cups in dissolved denture tablets.
- Poor some bicarbonate of soda into the cup and clean. Scrunched up aluminium foil can be used as a scourer if needed.

Water marks on wood

- Always use coasters, especially with hot drinks, to avoid those horrible, white, water mark rings.
- A solution of half white vinegar and half olive oil rubbed into the wood can help eradicate the mark.
- Rub the flesh of a brazil nut over the stain.
- Use a solution of half lemon juice and half olive oil. Leave to absorb for a few hours before polishing.

Leather

I use value baby wipes on my cream leather sofa and it comes up a treat. If you want to treat and clean your sofa, you can buy saddle soap from equestrian centres, which is cheaper than consumer leather treatments, or you can make your own. Boil equal parts of linseed oil and white vinegar, and add 20 drops of your favourite essential oil. I like lavender or almond smells for leather. When cold, place in a container ready for use. Shake thoroughly before using and rub on with a soft cloth.

Candle wax spills

One of the easiest ways to remove candle wax from fabric or even carpets is to cover the area with brown paper and iron over. Make sure the paper is larger than the area you are treating to avoid scorching the carpet!

The Scented Home

There is nothing nicer than walking into a home that smells fresh and clean. We all get used to our individual smells and may not notice when things become a bit whiffy. Smokers, pet owners and people that fry a lot of food may not notice the smells that can build up in their homes. As with cleaning products, there are air fresheners lining the supermarket shelves. The problem is that most only mask the odours, and often that mask is a very artificial smell. Worryingly, some scientists believe there is a strong link between chemical air fresheners and some respiratory health problems.

Keep it clean

It is common sense, but a clean home will smell sweeter than a dirty home. Removing dust and grime will help rooms breathe.

A breath of fresh air

We live in central-heated homes with double-glazed windows. Some people only open their windows in the summer months. Think of all the stagnated air circulating around in your home! Get into the habit of opening windows, even for short periods, every day. Remember to turn the heat off in that room first to avoid wasting energy.

Scented candles

I am a big fan of scented candles, but you do get what you pay for. I have wasted far too much money on scented candles that smell terrible or burn inconsistently. My absolute favourite luxury candles are Neom Organics and Jo Malone, but I have to wait for a kind soul to buy these for me and then I only light them on special occasions! For everyday use, Yankee candles are great and last well. They have just introduced a 100% natural soy wax range. For budget ranges, Homebase have great pillar scented candles that burn well and give a subtle scent. Marks & Spencer's scented candles are also effective and good value. For stronger scents, you can opt for the supermarket favourites from Fabreze or Airwick.

Scented candles may appear expensive, but compare this to a house bulging with plug-ins, sprays and other lotions and potions and it will soon be offset. I don't have scented candles burning constantly, but tend to light them prior to visitors arriving, after a particularly 'smelly' meal or just to suit my mood. If you are creative, you can save money and make your own candles, using essential oils to fragrance them.

Carpet freshener

Whenever I think of carpet fresheners, my mind reverts to the TV advert with the manic lady doing the 'shake'n'vac' dance! You can make your own carpet freshener by sprinkling bicarbonate of soda over your carpets. Leave for 10 to 15 minutes and then vacuum. I have a large tub of bicarbonate of soda mixed with sachets of lavender and rose petals. The bicarb absorbs the scent of the petals to create my very own carpet freshener.

Fresh flowers and plants

Bring nature into your home. Certain plants absorb odours and help clean the air around you. Several plants have been identified by NASA as helping to eliminate toxins. Spider plant is said to be effective in removing formaldehyde from the air, or why not opt for a gerbera, peace lily or chrysanthemum to help keep the air a touch purer. A bunch of scented flowers can really brighten a room and create a welcoming scent. To save money, grow your own flowers, choosing the most scented varieties all year around.

Create a welcoming home

Estate agents have been using these tricks for years. The smell of freshly baked bread, home-baked cookies and fresh coffee is incredibly welcoming and makes the whole house smell divine.

Pets' corner

Pets can leave lingering odours, particularly dogs. Make sure the bedding is washed regularly to keep it fresh and clean. Dogs should be bathed regularly. If your dog is wet or dirty after a walk, keep it in a drying out area before giving it the run of the house.

Essential oils

If you like essential oils you can add your favourite scent to radiators and even light bulbs (using a light bulb ring) to help give off the fragrance. I also add drops to logs and the melted wax of cheaper scented candles. Potpourri refresher oils are also great, particularly for those special smells such as Christmas blends.

Loving your fresh drawers

Scented drawer liners and air fresheners can be expensive. You can achieve similar results by utilising home products.

- Place some bars of unused value soap in your drawers to help freshen. At the time of writing, I can buy three bars for less than 20p.
- Using scraps of fabric, make yourself a scented sack – no sewing required! Cut some fabric into a circle or square. Place a mixture of dried lavender and bicarbonate of soda in the middle of the fabric. Gather up the edges and tie securely with ribbon or string. Hang in wardrobes or place in drawers. For those who love sewing, why not make a scented heart? Cut out two heart shapes and sew around the edges leaving a 2 cm gap. Fill using a funnel. Finish by sewing together the remaining gap.

- Add drops of your favourite essential oil or perfume to scraps of ribbon. Hang the ribbon in the wardrobe or place in your drawers.
- Economy tumble drier sheets give off a fresh fragrance for three to four weeks and can be placed in drawers or even inside pillowcases to maintain freshness.

Gel air fresheners

You can make your own gel air fresheners, but keep them out of reach of young children in case they want to eat them. Place in decorative jars or shot glasses.

    1 litre of water
    Gelatine
    Essential oil
    Food colouring
    Glitter (optional but looks quite nice in shot glasses)

Boil the water in an old saucepan and add the gelatine until dissolved (check gelatine instructions to ensure the correct proportions needed to set the gel). Add 20 to 30 drops of your favourite essential oil, and the food colouring of your choice. Pour into your chosen jars or glasses and allow to set.

Nasty kitchen smells

Cooking can create some unpleasant smells. A simple solution is to boil equal parts of water and white vinegar. You can add some essential oils, cloves, cinnamon or citrus peel. Leave simmering for as long as possible, but don't allow to boil dry. The vinegar smell will disappear, along with the unwanted odours.

CHAPTER FOUR

Food and Drink

'NEVER EAT
MORE THAN YOU
CAN LIFT.'
Miss Piggy

A recent survey shown on BBC Breakfast (February 2009) claimed the cost of food and drink has risen by up to 18%, with meat and fish seeing the biggest rise. Store cupboard essentials, such as pasta and rice, have also risen. The average household spends £150 a week on groceries. Supermarkets are jumping over themselves to save us money, but are their deals really what they seem?

In addition to all the other problems we may have in the UK, the current recession is something that affects everyone. We are experiencing the biggest recession since the Second World War, with banks and governments in crisis, redundancies and a significant rise in unemployment. However, on the positive side, families are living a less materialistic lifestyle and statistics have shown that allotment gardening has never been more popular. These lifestyle changes will have a positive impact on our health and our environment.

My grandfather, if he were alive, would be telling me that it would be the making of this country. The last time the country was brought down to its knees was during the Second World War – and, yet, this was a time when we were fitter and healthier than we have ever been. Hard to believe when you think of food rationing and the extremes our ancestors had to put up with. Women ran the homes and believed it was their role as part of the war effort to make the food last and to provide healthy and hearty meals. We cannot recreate what happened during the war; our lives are not set up in the same way. Most families survive with both parents working and they do not have the time to devote to home making in the same way we did 60 years ago. However, there is still a lot to learn from our ancestors.

Unbelievably, almost a third of our weekly shop ends up in the dustbin. Fresh fruit, vegetables and dairy products create the most wastage. I have known families who buy fresh fruit and vegetables to make them feel healthier, but with no real desire to actually eat them! We have become a nation of buying what we fancy, when we fancy, with no real thought about what we are going to do with it when we get home. I am as guilty as the rest of you, often finding unused items tucked away in the back of my fridge, well past their sell-by-date.

I am not suggesting for a minute we go without food or stop those fabulous treats ... I certainly could not contemplate a life without my bar of Green & Black's chocolate. Instead, here are some tips to help your money last longer, keep your tummies fuller and, hopefully, help make a healthier and more contented you.

Getting the Right Equipment

It may sound strange, beginning this section with saving money and then asking you to spend it. You will have to trust me on this one. A little bit of time invested in this area can save you time and more importantly money later on! A word of warning, if you are not sure you or your family will use the items listed, don't buy them, or at least don't buy new or it may end up in the back of the cupboard along with the yoghurt maker and the singing fish ... all of which may have seemed like a good idea at the time!

If you don't have the money to buy the equipment and don't mind second hand, why not put a request on Freecycle (www.freecycle.org) or try to locate the item at your local bootsale, through eBay or a local paper.

Slow cooker

These are electric stockpots and are so very simple to use. If you are unsure what a stockpot is, it is simply a large pot for making soups, stews and casseroles. Find a recipe you like, and all you do is add your ingredients to the pot, turn it on and come back in six to eight hours to a perfect meal, with no effort from you! Best of all, because the ingredients are cooked slowly and below boiling point, the nutrients are not destroyed, so you save money and time, and you end up with a highly nutritious meal.

Bread makers

If you like the taste and smell of fresh bread, why not make it yourself. Bread makers are very simple to use and require no effort – just add the ingredients and press go. Most machines have a timer you can set up to 13 hours ahead to have your finished bread any time – it's wonderful to wake up in the morning to the smell of freshly baked bread! You can buy bread mixes from 40p a pack (for approximately a 1 lb loaf), or add your flour and yeast to create your own. This works out at half the price of fresh bread. A word of warning: if you are happy with value sliced white from the supermarket at 7p a loaf, a bread maker is not going to save you money.

Tiered steamer

Steamers are a great invention. Nutritionally, they give far superior results to boiling, which destroys the nutrients as they are leaked into the water. The taste is also noticeably better, but the most important factor for the budgeteer is that they can save you money. Why use three rings on your cooker for your vegetables, when this little gem cooks them all on one? You can buy a steamer for your hob, or you can buy an electric steamer, which is far advanced even knowing to turn off the vegetables at the right moment, keeping them warm but preventing them from going soggy. I am in awe! You can buy a three-in-one machine (Tefal do a great one), combining a stockpot, rice cooker and steamer. A fantastic investment.

A freezer

If you are planning to save money, a freezer is a great asset. You can fill it with bargains, food grown on your allotment and with homemade ready meals. Remember they work more efficiently when used, so fill it up but make a note of what is going in. If you are freezing home-produced items, label them with the contents and date. Remember, the bigger the freezer, the easier it is to lose track of the contents. If you're buying new, make sure you choose one with the best energy efficiency grading.

There are many gadgets and gizmos on the market claiming to save you money, save the environment, or ideally both. Don't buy unless you need them. If your fridge packs up and you have to replace it, then you should go for the best energy efficient model available to save you money, but if your fridge is working well, it would not be a great money saving tactic to go out and replace it.

Putting your House in Order

As much as we would like to think otherwise, the vast majority of us are unaware of what is lurking in our store cupboards, fridge and freezers. A friend of mine discovered a frozen chicken in her freezer that was eight years old! How can we possibly budget for food when we are unaware of what we have? We walk around super-markets in a trance-like state, picking things up more out of habit than need.

Making a list and checking it twice

When I started looking at my household food budgets, I decided to make a checklist of the key foods in my kitchen (not store cupboard essentials or snacks). I then made a list of all the meals I could make using these ingredients. I estimated I would have about five main meals. I was shocked; I managed 18 substantial meals and nine puddings. I thought it would be fun to write these meals down and tick them off when I had made them. I then created a shopping list by adding the key ingredients I needed to replace. It was a revelation. I did not have to think about what to cook; I simply went to my list and chose something I fancied. Over a fortnight, I cut my shopping bill by over a third without buying less or cheaper food.

Store cupboard essentials

Think of the television programme 'Ready Steady Cook' – a few key ingredients and you have a great meal, but not without some essential store cupboard favourites. The following are mine.

Must-haves

- Baked beans
- Rice
- Pasta
- Flour – plain and self-raising
- Sugar
- Tomato puree
- Red lentils
- Herbs and spices
- Garlic
- Oats
- Long-life, fresh or frozen milk
- Olive oil
- Stock cubes

Optional

- Readymade pasta or curry sauce (bought on offer!)
- Bread flour and dried yeast (so you can always make your own bread)
- Tinned tuna
- Dried fruit
- Passata (sieved tomatoes)

Vegetable rack

- Potatoes

- Onions
- Carrots
- Garlic

Fridge store
- Cheese
- Eggs
- Milk
- Butter or margarine
- Natural yoghurt

Freezer store
- Peas or other vegetables as standby
- Puff pastry
- Mince
- Two loaves of bread and/or bread rolls
- Sausages
- Frozen herbs

I always make sure that these items are topped up. Just looking at that list I could, in an emergency, make several meals.

Great Food Ideas

Ditch the junk
You don't have to be a budding Jamie Oliver to cook delicious food. As hard as it may seem to those who love nothing better than slamming a ready meal in the microwave, home-cooked fresh food can actually be quite quick to

prepare and very simple. If you don't know where to start, buy a recipe book designed for novices – there are some great ones available. Creating your own food can be so rewarding and very relaxing and, most importantly, it saves you money!

Herbs

If you love cooking, you probably buy fresh herbs. It is wonderful if you can grow herbs in your own pots or garden, as if you are buying them fresh from the supermarket you may be paying a premium. If you can't grow your own, or it is the wrong time of year, one great product I have recently tried is frozen herbs. For the same price as fresh herbs, you can buy a large container of freshly frozen herbs that can last you months and offer a superior taste over dried varieties. Waitrose sell 75g re-sealable bags of herbs and seasonings. Simply use what you want and pop the rest back into the freezer.

Bake one, bake one free

My mum would never use the oven unless she could fill it up. If you are baking or being creative in the kitchen, why not double up and make more? You can then freeze one, saving you time, energy and money. This is great for everyone, whether you are a single person or a family of four.

Get your fill

One of the most expensive items on our shopping lists is snack food. We eat out of boredom or other emotional incentive, and often we confuse thirst pangs for hunger pangs. One of the best ways to avoid snacking is to fill up on energy-giving foods at meal times.

Try to eat muesli or porridge oats for breakfast or, if you have your own chickens, why not a poached egg on wholemeal toast? Whatever it is you want to eat, ensure it is not empty food. Breakfast cereals, particularly those aimed at children, are expensive, full of sugar and contain very little nutrients – yet we still buy them.

Soups and casseroles (that utilise your fabulous stockpot) are highly nutritious. Why not add some nutritious red lentils to your existing casserole recipe. These don't need soaking. They are cheap and packed with essential nutrients. They also help bulk a meal, making it last longer, and can be used as a thickener.

By changing our eating habits we can save money, improve our health and, if needed, even lose weight.

Wake up and smell the coffee

With cafés and coffee shops on every street corner, it is very tempting to pop in for elevenses or for a bite of lunch. I looked over my bank statements for a few months last year when the office I was working at had limited kitchen facilities. I was shocked. I had spent on average £50 a week on lunches and snacks. If you add on top of this take-away drinks and snacks, the sum can be frightening. How many of you nip into their nearest coffee house to bring back take-out coffee rather than use the office coffee machine? Add that up over a week or a month and you will be stunned. A friend of mine decided to cut out her take-out fix and instead, whenever the other girls in the office went out to buy, she put the money in a jar on her desk. Within a month, she had enough to buy herself a pair of gorgeous shoes she had her eye on.

Fill your lunch box

It only takes a few minutes every day to sort out a nice packed lunch. If you still don't have the incentive to do this, try asking your employer if they will give you facilities to make your own food. We have a stockpot in our office. We all put money into a kitty and every morning we take it in turns to make the soup. By lunchtime, the smell of homemade soup is enough to stop us wanting to go to the nearest sandwich bar.

Look After Your Fruit and Vegetables

As we already know, we waste more fruit and vegetables than any other item on our grocery lists. Here are some tips to avoid waste.

Buy what you need

If you are able to buy fresh fruit and vegetables regularly, buy as and when needed. This will avoid waste and ensure you eat lovely fresh produce every day while saving money.

Storage

Think about where you are storing your fruit and vegetables. Traditionally, homes had a cool pantry or larder, which was perfect for keeping things fresh. Apples were stored to last the whole winter, yet we struggle to get them to last a week. Supermarkets may have had the produce for weeks before it reaches you, thereby shortening its life, so it is always best to buy from your local farmers' market, pannier market or greengrocer.

Bananas

If you want them to last, buy them green. Never store bananas in the fridge, but do try to keep them in a cool place and not touching other fruit as they omit a gas that speeds up the ripening process.

Mushrooms

Although most supermarkets sell mushrooms in those horrible plastic containers, they should be placed in paper bags and stored in the fridge. The plastic bags produce moisture and the mushrooms will start to decay and rot very quickly.

Root vegetables

Keep root vegetables in a dry, cool, dark place. If you do not have an area suitable, store them in your fridge but not in the plastic packaging. Placing an old tea towel on the base of the fridge shelf will avoid moisture. Potatoes love dark, cool places. Never leave them in plastic, though paper bags are fine.

Salad produce

Bagged salads are very expensive as well as damaging to the environment. Out of season, buy lettuce whole (iceberg seems to be the longest lasting). Store all salad items in your fridge, out of plastic and away from moisture. Again, you can use the tea towel trick. Why not grow your own lettuce or tomatoes? Lettuce can be grown in window boxes or grow your own tomatoes in grow bags on your patio. Cucumbers and tomatoes should be eaten firm. If you like the tomatoes with lots of flavour, place them in a bowl at room temperature. They will only last three to four days but will be very tasty.

Fruit

As with vegetables, store fruit in a cool, dry place. This sounds obvious, but I have walked into houses with fruit bowls next to radiators or in front of windows. If you prefer, store fruit in the fridge although keep apples away from any fruit or vegetables you want to preserve as apples produce ethylene which speeds up the ripening process.

Strawberries

Strawberries never taste the same out of season. Never buy punnets containing mouldy fruit, as this will speed up the ripening process of the other fruits. Store in the fridge until you are ready to eat them, but remember to take them out at least an hour before serving as this improves the flavour.

Money Saving Tips for Grocery Shopping

Now that we have the basics sorted out at home, we can concentrate on looking for the bargains.

Be prepared

Always, always, always make a list before shopping. This will help keep you focused and less likely to buy unwanted items or double up on what you already have. I cannot emphasise this enough. You can save pounds every week by being organised and following your list. If you only take one thing from this chapter, please let it be the list making!

Buy with your head, not your stomach

Never go shopping when you are hungry. It is a sure-fire way to spend more money. As you are wandering around the supermarket in a trance-like state, you will get to the checkout and wonder why your trolley is heaving with crisps, chocolate and biscuits. Have you wondered why supermarkets have started baking bread on the premises? Not to give us the freshest bread (most is just reheated anyway!), but simply to create that mouth-watering smell to tempt us into buying.

BOGOF deals

'Buy one get one free' can seem like a great deal, but only if you were intending to buy the product in the first place. Before you buy, remember to compare the price. You may find you are paying more than double when compared to other brands. Don't be fooled into thinking that the man-ufacturers or supermarkets are offering a free item out of the goodness of their hearts. It is purely a marketing tool to lure us into buying products we may not normally buy, or to help launch a new range. So, the golden rule: only buy if it saves you money, is something you need and something you will use.

B2GOF deals

'Buy two get one free' are often trick deals, lulling you into a false sense of money saving! I have succumbed to buying three items of something I would not normally buy, simply because I was sucked into thinking it was a great deal. On some occasions, I have discovered the items were dramatically cheaper elsewhere and I had not saved much, if any, money at all – I had just spent more of my weekly budget. B2GOF deals are popular at Christmas. I have spent hours wandering around the store trying to find the elusive third item, while mentally trying to work out the best value for the free item – all of which inevitably means I spend more money. It can get so confusing you feel like you need a maths degree just to sort it all out.

My advice is to be very careful. Remember the golden rule: do you want it, will you use it and is it really saving you money? If you answer yes to all three, then go ahead. If in doubt, walk away.

BOGO ½ price

As advised above, only buy these 'buy one get one half price' deals if you believe you are saving money and actually want and need the item. I tend only to opt for these deals if it is a store essential or something I use week in week out.

Money-off coupons

Coupons are a great source of saving money. You can collect them online or pick up the supermarket magazines (normally free at the checkout) as these will be packed with coupons. In some cases, supermarkets may accept coupons even if you have not purchased the item though they are not obliged to do so.

Loyalty cards

Most supermarkets offer loyalty cards. It is a good idea to use them as the points soon build up. Spend some time looking at the shop's loyalty card offers as often you get more for your money utilising the offers than if you used them to discount your food shop. Some people have become experts in loyalty cards, buying products with extra points and redeeming them against larger items, saving pounds. Money saving forums are great for highlighting current offers and any legal loopholes.

Downshifting

Martin Lewis (www.moneysavingexpert.com) is a powerful advocate of downshifting and believes you can shave 33% off your food bills. I like his advice. Downshifting does not always mean jumping from a premium brand straight to a no frills product; you can look at the middle of the range products on the shelf. I have noticed no difference for a number of value items – such as dried pasta, flour, butter and even some biscuits. It is all personal taste. As Martin recommends, if you normally buy four tins of baked beans a week, start off by buying three of your normal brand and one of the no frills. That way, if you don't like the no frills, you have not wasted the money.

Don't just look at food items – you can save money on toiletries, skin care and cleaning products. One skin care product that springs to mind is the anti-ageing day and night creams from Aldi. Priced at only £1.89 a pot, these creams come top in many surveys, beating market leaders such as L'Oreal, Olay and even Crème de la Mer!

Case study

Andrew and I have been at rock bottom financially for over 12 months with no savings to help us. Yet we still enjoy life and make our own fun. We have enjoyed going back to basics with good home cooking – and I don't just mean basic meals. We live well; we just buy wisely. Our children really still have no idea to this day that things have been so tight over this period and I think they are happier than ever. We have games nights, summer picnics in our garden with basic games such as rounders and tin can squash with an empty tin can. There are lots of fun free games and things to do and we have all loved it and are even closer than ever.

We buy potatoes in sacks, rather than in smaller bags, and have found this saves so much money. We also buy food in the 'buy it now' section of the supermarket, which is usually going past its sell-by date that day or the next day. These items sell at less than quarter of the original price in many instances. We went from buying Warburtons bread at £1.48 a loaf to buying Morrisons value bread at 19p a loaf. Being a family of seven, that was a massive saving and it didn't turn out to be compromise at all, as the Morrisons bread is genuinely just as fresh and tasty as the Warburtons.

My children love noodles. Batchelors Chicken and Mushroom noodles are 48p per pack; Asda do exactly the same type of noodles for 8p per pack. The price difference is amazing and it's exactly the same product. Once, as I was filling my basket with Asda noodles at 8p a packet, a man next to me was putting in his trolley several packs of Batchelors noodles at 48p a pack. I wanted to scream and shout at him saying, 'what are you doing?' It's like throwing 40p a pack into the bin on your way out. Some people are blinded by the branded products and have no regard for the amount of money they throw away each day.

'Convenience food' – I still have no idea how people are able to shop this way, despite the fact that is a very unhealthy and unimaginative way to eat. Home cooking from raw ingredients is far more cost effective, much tastier and far more imaginative than any pre-packed convenience food.

Being on a budget doesn't mean unhappiness; it just means that you have to think differently.

Read the small print

Have you ever looked at the supermarket shelf labels? They are a good way to assess if you really are getting a great deal. Each shelf label should give you the item's price or quantity per weight. For example, comparing two leading brands of cat food, both packs may be £4, but when I look at the shelf label I notice that one contains only 750g and the other 1 kg, making the price per gram significantly cheaper in one brand than the other. It is always worth reading these labels even when considering a sale item or BOGOF deal. You will be surprised at the results.

Webwise

You can now order your groceries from the comfort of your own home and have them delivered straight to your door. There is usually a charge for delivery (£5 on average) but, if this works out to be cheaper than using your own car, why not opt for it? Another great asset of shopping online is that you are less likely to overspend or fall foul to the pester power tricks of the supermarket.

If you have time on your hands, why not look at some comparison sites that specialise in supermarket shopping such as www.mysupermarket.co.uk

Join a local co-op scheme

In many areas you will find a local co-op scheme (if not, why not start one?). A cooperative scheme works by getting a few households and friends together to buy items in bulk and at wholesale prices, which you then distribute amongst yourselves, therefore saving money. I run a co-op for organic and health foods through Essential Trading in Bristol. Health foods and organic items tend to be much more expensive than non-organic items, particularly the no-frills versions, but I personally like to buy organic and this is the best way for me to do so and save some money.

Farmers' markets

If you love fresh produce, you will enjoy a farmer's market. There are over 500 farmers' markets across the UK, so you should find one near you. I love the atmosphere, the smell and the ability to taste my way around the market (as many stallholders have little gems of food samples to tempt you!). It is great to support your local economy.

The Good Life

Many articles on money saving advise lifestyle changes. In an ideal world, we will all have time to live better lives for the environment and ourselves. Until then, we have to do what we can. I firmly believe that our time is almost as valuable as money. I am a 'good life' dipper rather than a full-time domestic goddess. The secret is to do what appeals. You must enjoy your life so, if the idea of digging a garden fills you with dread, it's better to focus on finding a local farmer's market instead.

Grow your own

If you have access to a garden or allotment and the time to maintain it, growing your own can be a fantastic hobby. It can save you money and, if you have any surplus to your own requirements, you could sell your produce to your friends and neighbours. Growing your own is incredibly rewarding but it is very time consuming, back breaking and at times tedious work. You need to dedicate time, energy and money getting the garden straight before you start to reap any rewards. Personally, I think there is nothing nicer than eating potatoes straight out of the ground or tomatoes off the vine, although I have to be motivated to get into the garden when it is cold and wet.

If you like the idea of a garden but have limited time, why not speak to friends or neighbours to see if they want to share your garden or allotment. This is a great motivator. You will be sharing the cost, time and effort, and will still have enough produce to share amongst you.

I could fill pages and pages on how to garden but I am not an expert. There are many books on the market to help new gardeners, so I will leave the words of wisdom to others. One book I found inspiring is *The Lazy Kitchen Gardener* by John Yeoman. It does what it says on the tin and lazy beings like me can plant and grow vegetables with the minimum of effort – a man after my own heart. The other is *How to Grow Your Own Food* by Dirty Nails. It is very simple to follow and gives you a no-nonsense week-by-week guide on what to plant and how to look after it.

Home brewing

If you enjoy a tipple, why not consider brewing your own? Kits are better, faster and tastier than they have ever been. You can save up to 50% on wines and beers. Once brewed, turn them into fabulous homemade gifts for your friends and families.

Jam and chutney making

If you have a garden bulging with berries, you could try making homemade jam. It is not a cheap alternative if you have to buy the fruit and the sugar is quite expensive, but for those using what grows in the garden, it can be very rewarding. Chutney is great for using up green tomatoes or other items from your garden. Decorate the jars with some scraps of fabric and pretty labels and they will make wonderful gifts. Collect your old jars ready to reuse.

If you are concerned about mastering the art of making jam, you can always buy a jam maker. Tefal offer the Vitafruit electric jam maker but it is quite expensive at £79 so make sure you will use it before you buy, as that is an awful lot of jam!

Livestock

You might consider keeping your own chickens, ducks or even pigs (if your garden allows). Chickens are great for fresh eggs and getting the children involved. As a vegetarian, I personally could not kill them for food but that would be your choice. You can get laying hens, less than a year old, from the Battery Hen Welfare Trust (www.bhwt.org.uk) for as little as 50p each. Intensive chicken farmers allow the Trust to take their chickens for nothing when they are going to clear out their batteries and they find good homes for them. It is a joy to watch these chickens stretch their legs for the first time. The minimum number of chickens you can take is three, in case one dies. If you are worried about encouraging vermin, why not opt for the fabulous and stylish Omlet Eglu? (See www.omlet.co.uk)

Case study

Carol Farley has chickens. She shares here some wise words of wisdom.

The chickens were my birthday present from my husband last summer but the cost for keeping them was initially quite steep. Starting from absolute scratch it has cost us:

• £400 for the henhouse (from the Domestic Fowl

Trust) but there are cheaper options.

- £15 per hen/cockerel.
- £25 for the feeders/drinkers (purchased from a local country auction).
- Approximately £12 a month for feed and upkeep (layers pellets, corn, worming treatment, dried mealworms, wood shavings, a squirt of disinfectant or red spider mite powder).
- We have just bought some electric fencing to make a large run in the garden. The chickens were allowed to be free ranging but, unfortunately, the foxes have taken two of them in five months, so that's cost another £400 with all the bits.

Apart from that, there are no other costs for food as they eat the scraps and any veg from the veg box that isn't eaten by us – they love a brussels stalk. It takes literally five minutes in the morning to freshen their water and put the feed out, five minutes a day to clear the poo out of the henhouse and let them out into the run, and then about 15 minutes once a week to clean out the henhouse totally and replenish the wood shavings. But you gain hours and hours of fun watching them scratch around and forage together as a little team. This watching also helps you to discover their individual little personalities too.

The benefits for the money saving family are:
- Hen poo makes good manure for the garden.
- They scratch around the garden and help to scarify the lawn.

- They provide eggs.
- They are fabulous to have around.

  The negatives are:
- They are not cost-effective unless you run them as a business rather than as pets.
- They have to be protected from foxes.
- You have to make sure that someone is around at their 'bedtime' to make sure that their door into their bedroom is closed. This just in case any predators were to get in and also to protect them from the elements during the night.

Overall, we are absolutely delighted we made the decision to get them.

CHAPTER FIVE

Recipes

'THERE IS NO LOVE SINCERER
THAN THE LOVE OF FOOD.'
George Bernard Shaw

One of the keys to effective money saving in the home is the ability to cook your own food. Processed food is far more expensive than cooking from scratch. You don't have to be the next Jamie Oliver to make your own meals. Cooking is simple, fun and addictive. Teach your children to cook with you – these life-skills are invaluable for their health and their financial future.

Invest in a good cookery book to suit your taste. Gill Holcombe's *How to feed your whole family a healthy balanced diet with very little money ... and hardly any time, even if you have a tiny kitchen, only three saucepans (one with an ill-fitting lid) and no fancy gadgets – unless you count the garlic crusher...* is a great family book for the budgeter. Other classics include Jamie Oliver's *Ministry of Food*, Delia Smith's *How to Cook* and *Frugal Food*.

If you like going online, why not have a look at www.bbcgoodfood.com This website has a tab 'How to Cook' where you can watch videos and follow step-by-step instructions. Alternatively, why not join an evening class? You will soon find cooking can become quite addictive. My dad has recently retired. He has discovered a whole new world and spends hours reading recipe books. He is quite confident now and is even making his own adaptations to the recipes.

We have already sorted out your store cupboard essentials, so now we need to concentrate on some key recipes to help you on your way. I have included a few recipes for the basics, meat, fish, vegetarian and, the most exciting for me, baking. Have a look at the vegetarian recipes, even if you are an ardent meat eater – you may find some surprises. I have included many soup recipes in the vegetarian section. With a little bit of imagination and some culinary magic, you can transfer these recipes into meat soups or casseroles. Simply add your desired ingredient and hey presto! The vegetable soup is a great example. Add some chicken and you will have a wholesome vegetable and chicken broth – perfect when you are feeling low.

I have included rough prices with each dish. These were taken from www.moneysupermarket.com at the time of writing.

The Basics

Whether you are a vegetarian or a meat eater, some of the basic principles of cooking and following recipes remain the same. Here are some quick and easy recipes suitable for both lifestyles.

Basic bolognaise mince

Costs less than £2 for four servings

This recipe can be made using a 'cheat' ingredient of bolognaise or pasta sauce or, if you are feeling adventurous, make your own.

> 2 or 3 cloves of garlic, finely chopped
> 1 onion, finely chopped
> 1 pepper, finely chopped (optional)
> 1 lb mince meat or, for vegetarians, veggie mince
> 1 tin chopped tomatoes
> 150ml red wine
> Mixed herbs to taste

1. Fry the onion and garlic in a pan until soft and translucent.
2. Add the mince and cook until brown.
3. Add the tomatoes stirring well and add wine and herbs to taste.
4. Leave to simmer for 5 minutes.

This sauce can be used as a basic bolognaise sauce, served with spaghetti and garnished with parmesan.

Alternatively, the same base can be used to make a lasagne. Simply alternate with a layer of mince, white sauce and lasagne sheets, finishing with a layer of white sauce. Bake in a moderate oven for 35–40 minutes. The same principle applies for cannelloni or moussaka.

If you want to make a shepherd's pie, add gravy granules, Marmite or Worcester sauce to the mince. Cover the mince with fluffy mashed potato and a sprinkle of grated cheese before baking.

Savoury pastry

200g white or wholegrain plain flour (use granary flour if you like seedy pastry)
100g cold butter or margarine
Cold water

1. Place the flour in a bowl.
2. Cut the butter into cubes and add to the flour.
3. Using your fingertips, gently rub the butter into the flour to form breadcrumbs.
4. Add cold water until you form a firm pastry dough. Try to avoid handling the dough too much as pastry does not like heat. If you are concerned, place the pastry in the fridge to cool until ready to use.

For speed, I use a food processor to make my pastry. Put the flour and butter into the bowl, whizz and gradually add cold water until a ball of dough is formed. Simple and no mess.

Use this pastry to make quiche, savoury tarts or sausage rolls.

Sweet pastry

This is a recipe I use for Christmas mince pies or apple pies (see the recipe in the Baking section below), but feel free to adapt it to suit your own taste. I find sweet pastry far better to make in a food processor.

> 200g white plain flour
> 100g butter
> 1–2 tsp cinnamon
> 3 heaped tsp icing sugar
> Orange juice

1. Place flour, icing sugar and cinnamon in a bowl.
2. Add cubes of butter. Using your fingertips, gently rub the butter into the flour to form breadcrumbs.
3. Add cold orange juice until you form a firm pastry dough. Try to avoid handling the dough too much as pastry does not like heat. If you are concerned, place the pastry in the fridge to cool until ready to use.

For speed, I use a food processor to make my pastry. Put the flour, icing sugar, cinnamon and butter into the bowl, whizz and gradually add the cold orange juice until a ball of dough is formed. I let this dough rest for five minutes in the fridge before using.

Basic pasta sauce
Costs less than £1

This is a great base for many recipes. You can use it on its own for a traditional pasta sauce, add it to a casserole or meatballs (see recipe in the following Meat section) or even use as a pizza topping. I am sure you can think of lots more recipes and variations!

    1 or 2 cloves of garlic, chopped
    1 onion, chopped
    ½ red pepper, chopped
    150g tomatoes, chopped (In season, it is nice to get a selection
    of different tomatoes to add a variety of flavours. You can
    substitute fresh tomatoes for tinned.)
    100ml red wine (optional)
    Italian herbs to flavour

1. Fry the onion and garlic in a pan until translucent.
2. Add the pepper and cook for 2–3 minutes.
3. Add tomatoes, red wine and herbs.
4. Season to taste.

You can vary this recipe by adding some spices (chilli is good), mushrooms, spinach, basil leaves or chopped mozzarella just before serving. For a creamy sauce, add half a tub of crème fraîche.

Basic white sauce

Mastering the art of making your own white sauce saves money and nothing beats the taste of fresh sauces. Add cheese to make macaroni or cauliflower cheese. Add parsley and serve with ham or fish. This sauce can be made with soya milk and dairy-free spread for those who wish to be dairy free.

> 25g plain flour or cornflour
> 25g butter
> Milk
> Seasoning to taste

1. Melt the butter.

2. Add flour and stir with a wooden spoon until it starts to thicken.

3. Add the milk a little at a time to avoid lumps. Change to a hand whisk to avoid lumps, stirring continually.

4. As the sauce begins to thicken, add milk until it reaches the desired consistency.

5. Season to taste.

6. If you're making a cheese sauce, add grated cheese and ½ tsp of mustard.

Top tip!

When making cheese sauce, use mature cheese as you need less. Nutritional yeast flakes, by Marigold, give a cheesy taste to sauces and are suitable for vegans.

Delicious roast potatoes

Large potatoes
Oil of your choice (I use sunflower oil)
3–4 tsp semolina
Paprika

1. Peel and cut large potatoes ready to roast.
2. Steam or boil the potatoes for 10 minutes.
3. While the potatoes are cooking, add oil to a roasting tin (about an inch depth) and place in a very hot oven.
4. Drain the potatoes and place them back into the saucepan.
5. Sprinkle the semolina and 2–3 tsp of paprika onto the potatoes.
6. Put the lid onto the saucepan and shake the potatoes for a few seconds.
7. Add the potatoes to the hot roasting oil, being careful not to splash.
8. Roast for 1–1½ hours at 200°C, turning the potatoes regularly to ensure a crispy coating. When turning, add more paprika.

Meat

I am not a meat eater, but I come from a family of meat eaters and farmers so I have begged favours and advice from them for this section. Here are some money-saving tips when choosing your meat courtesy of my mum!

Speak to your local butcher and opt for cheaper cuts of meat. They should be able to advise you on the best deals and offers available and even give you some great tips on how to cook them.

Make the most of the purchase. For example, roast a whole chicken for one meal, use leftover meat in a pie for the next meal and then sandwiches or a cold salad thereafter.

Mince is wonderful for a number of meals – bolognaise, shepherd's pie or even a chilli.

If you're making a stew or casserole, choose cheaper cuts such as brisket, shanks or even shoulder. Cooked slowly, they can produce flavoursome and tender cooked meats. Stewing steak or skirt provides the most flavour but requires the longest cooking times. Dice and mix these cuts with vegetables and stock. Try cooking double the amount to make two meals – serve half with dumplings and half with sliced potato and grated cheese on top to make a hotpot.

Boiling gammon slipper or shoulder is cheaper than a whole gammon joint and still lean. Cook for 20 minutes per pound. Boil, bake or slow cook to produce tender meat. Serve with egg and chips, or with parsley sauce and sautéed or mashed potatoes. Any leftovers can be chopped to make sandwiches, pies or a quiche.

Italian style meatballs
Costs £1.75 for four servings

Basic pasta sauce (see recipe in the Basics section above)
1 onion, finely chopped
450g lean mince
1 egg, beaten
Italian herbs to flavour
1 tbsp vegetable oil

1. In a bowl, mix together the mince, onion, herbs and egg.

2. Shape into 12 balls (meatballs can be frozen until ready to use).

3. Heat oil in a deep frying pan. Cook the balls for approximately 15 minutes until golden.

4. Pour over the pasta sauce and cook for a further 5 minutes until ready to serve on a bed of spaghetti.

Homemade chicken nuggets
Costs from £3.40 for four servings
Four skinless and boneless chicken fillets

> 3–4 tsp chicken seasoning
>
> 4 tbsp plain flour
>
> 2 tsp paprika
>
> 100g breadcrumbs (made from your leftover bread)
>
> 2 eggs, beaten
>
> Olive oil spray (place olive oil into a spray container – don't buy sprays as they are expensive)

1. Cut the fillets into the required size for nuggets.
2. You will need three bowls. In the first bowl mix the flour, seasoning and paprika. Pour the beaten eggs into the second bowl. Put the breadcrumbs into the third bowl.
3. Dip the chicken into the flour mix, ensuring all sides are coated. Then dip the floured chicken into the egg, again ensuring each piece is well coated. Then follow with the breadcrumbs.
4. Place the coated chicken onto a greased baking tray.
5. Spray with olive oil and bake for 20 minutes until golden in a hot oven.
6. Serve with homemade potato wedges.

Left-over chicken pie
Costs less than £3 for four servings

Cooked chicken removed from the bone
100g cooked ham (optional)
1 onion, chopped
50g mushrooms, quartered
2 sticks of celery, chopped
1 can chicken or mushroom condensed soup
Savoury or puff pastry

1. Fry the onion in a pan.
2. Add the celery, mushroom and cooked chicken and cook for 3–4 minutes.
3. Add the can of chicken or mushroom soup and heat for a further 3 minutes.
4. Place in a pie dish and cover with pastry or, if you're in a hurry, ready-made puff pastry.
5. Bake in the oven at 200°C for 30 minutes.

Fish

Fish is very nutritious and healthy. Oily fish is particularly good for you, so try to include it in your diet.

Creamy fish pie
Costs less than £3 for four servings

> 800g fish fillets, or ask your fishmonger for bits of flaky white fish
> 200g salmon pieces (optional)
> 100g prawns (optional)
> 1 tsp mustard
> 250ml milk
> 25g flour
> 25g butter
> 1kg potatoes
> Cheese

1. Boil or steam the potatoes until tender. Once they're cooked, mash ready for use.
2. Meanwhile, place the fish and milk in a pan and bring to the boil. Cook for 10 minutes or until the fish is cooked through.
3. Drain the fish and retain the liquid for making the creamy sauce.
4. Shred the fish ready for use and place in the pie dish.
5. Melt the butter in a pan and add the flour. Stir in the milk stock and thicken.
6. Add mustard, season and stir well. Pour over the fish.
7. Cover with mashed potato and with a final topping of grated cheese.
8. Bake in a moderate oven for 30 minutes.

Salmon fish cakes
Costs from £2.25 for four servings

400g fresh or tinned salmon
400g mashed potato
1–2 tbsp dill
2 tsp lemon juice
2 eggs, beaten
Plain flour

1. Mix the fish, potato, lemon juice and dill together in a bowl. Add almost all of the egg to bind, retaining a very small amount for brushing over the cakes later.
2. Form the mixture into cakes.
3. Place in the fridge to chill for 5 minutes.
4. Brush the remaining egg onto the cakes and dust with flour to coat.
5. Fry gently on both sides until golden.

Lemon and herb pan-fried cod
Costs less than £4 for four servings

4 cod fillets

50g wholemeal breadcrumbs (made from your leftover bread)

2 tbsp chopped parsley

1 tsp dill

Juice and rind of 1 lemon

Black pepper

50g butter

Olive oil

1. Mix together the breadcrumbs, herbs and lemon rind in a bowl and put to one side.

2. Place the cod fillets in a pan and fry both sides until tender (3–4 minutes).

3. Sprinkle the breadcrumb mix onto the fillets.

4. Place the pan under the grill to brown for 3 minutes.

5. Add the butter and lemon juice to the pan and melt for 1 minute.

6. Serve immediately spooning the butter over the fillets.

Vegetarian

Vegetarian meals are becoming increasingly popular as people cut back on their meat consumption. Here are some quick and easy favourites.

Goat's cheese and red onion tarts
Costs from £1.20 for four servings

You could make your own savoury pastry (see the recipe in the Basics section above) or buy a block of puff pastry and roll out. Bought pastry is more expensive so buy a supermarket-own brand that is frozen, not the ready-to-roll refrigerated pastry sheets.

200g pastry
1 large red onion, sliced
125g goat's cheese
Balsamic vinegar
Olive oil
2–3 tsp sugar
Black pepper

1. Place the onion in a pan with a little oil. Cook until soft.
2. Add balsamic vinegar and sugar, and cook on a low heat until the onion begins to caramelise. Don't let it burn!
3. If you're using savoury pastry, you can fill individual tart cases or one large flan case. If you're using puff pastry, simply roll out to the desired thickness and place the ingredients into the middle of the pastry, leaving at least ½ an inch around the outside of the pastry. This will naturally form a crust when baking.
4. Fill the cases with a layer of red onion, followed by crumbled goat's cheese and garnish with black pepper.
Bake in a moderate oven for 15–20 minutes until golden.

Spinach and ricotta lasagne
Costs less than £3 for four servings

1 onion, finely chopped
1 pot of ricotta
200–300g mature cheddar, grated
Fresh nutmeg, grated
Seasoning to taste
½ bag of spinach (baby leaf is best), washed
Pasta sauce (see recipe in the Basics section above)
No-precook lasagne sheets

1. In a bowl mix the onion, ricotta and cheddar together, retaining a small amount of cheddar to garnish later.
2. In a colander, run washed spinach under a hot tap for a few seconds to soften the leaves.
3. Add the spinach leaves to the ricotta mix.
4. Season and add a sprinkle of grated nutmeg.
5. In a lasagne dish, place a layer of the ricotta mix, followed by a layer of pasta sauce, followed by lasagne sheets.
6. Repeat, finishing with a layer of pasta sauce.
7. Add the grated cheese on top to finish.
8. Bake in a moderate oven for 40 minutes, until golden.
9. Serve with salad and new potatoes.

Mushroom and cashew nut roast

Costs £2.95 for six servings

This dish is made so much easier if you have a food processor that chops food. I can make this in minutes; otherwise you will drive yourself nuts (excuse the pun!) with all that chopping. I have many friends who are meat eaters and they all love this recipe. This dish can be frozen and used when needed.

> 1 onion, finely chopped
> 200g cashew nuts, chopped
> 250g mushrooms (I prefer chestnut mushrooms but choose whatever works for you)
> 100g breadcrumbs (made from your own bread)
> 2 tsp yeast extract

1. Fry the onion in a little oil until translucent.
2. Add the onions and nuts and cook for five minutes.
3. Add the yeast extract, followed by the breadcrumbs.
4. Place into a lined loaf tin and press down to form a firm base.
5. Bake at 180°C for 40 minutes.

Soups

Here are some soup recipes, perfect for slow cookers. You can use some soup recipes as a base for casseroles by simply including additional ingredients. For vegetarians, keep the ingredients chunky. For health purposes, I always cook my soups slowly as this retains all the nutrients. I don't bother cooking onions etc first. I have tried this and to be honest there is no difference in taste, so for speed and convenience I literally add all ingredients and get on with my life. Six hours later, I come back to a wholesome and yummy soup or casserole.

Pasta-less minestrone soup
Costs £1.95 for four servings

100g red kidney beans (cooked or tinned)
1 large onion, chopped
1 clove of garlic, crushed
1 carrot, diced
½ red pepper, chopped
400g tomatoes, chopped (fresh or tinned)
100g cabbage, shredded
100g fresh green beans, chopped
900ml vegetable stock
Tomato puree to taste (optional)
½ tsp cayenne pepper
2 bay leaves
1 tbsp fresh basil

1. Place all ingredients except the cabbage and basil into a slow cooker or large pan and cook slowly on a low heat for 2 hours (or longer if in a slow cooker).

2. Add the basil and shredded cabbage 20 minutes before serving.

3. Serve with crusty bread and hummus.

Rich vegetable soup

Costs £1.70 for four servings
This recipe can also work as a casserole if left chunky.

> 1 medium onion, coarsely chopped
> ½ swede, cubed
> 2 sweet potatoes, cubed
> 3 medium tomatoes, chopped
> 2 small carrots, chopped
> 1 small celery stalk with leaves, chopped
> 1 small apple, chopped
> 900ml stock or water
> 100ml apple juice
> ½ tsp dried dill
> 1 tbsp chopped parsley
> 1½ tsp paprika
> Dash of cayenne pepper

1. Prepare and place all ingredients into a slow cooker or a large saucepan.

2. Cook on a low heat for 1½–2 hours in a pan or 6 hours in a slow cooker.

3. Garnish with chopped parsley.

Carrot and coriander soup
Costs £1.50 for four servings

350g carrots, diced
100g celery or celeriac, diced
1 onion
1 clove of garlic
2 tsp ground coriander
1 tsp ground cumin
700–900ml vegetable stock or water
Salt and pepper (optional)
1 tsp finely chopped coriander leaves (optional)

1. Fry the onion and spices for 1 minute.
2. Add all ingredients and leave to cook on a low heat for 1½ hours, or cook in a slow cooker for 4–6 hours.
3. Liquidise the soup. Season to taste.
4. Add the chopped coriander leaves and serve hot.

Carrot, tomato and lentil soup
Costs £1.30 for four servings

3 medium carrots, chopped
1 large onion
400g tomatoes, chopped
125g lentils, washed
Tomato puree (optional)
½ red pepper
570ml stock or water
1 bay leaf
1 tsp basil or bunch fresh basil, chopped

1. Chop all vegetables and herbs and place in a heavy saucepan or slow cooker.
2. Cover with water and cook slowly for 1½ hours, or 4–6 hours in a slow cooker.
3. Liquidise and serve garnished with chopped basil.

Baking

There is nothing nicer than the smell of freshly baked bread or cakes. I love baking and often fantasise about running a little tea room. You don't have to be a great baker; here are some foolproof recipes to help you on your way. As with most things in life, practice makes perfect. The more you bake the better you will become. The most important factor is to enjoy the experience.

Yummy apple pie with sweet cinnamon pastry
£1.75 for six servings

> Sweet pastry (see recipe in the Basics section above)
> 3–4 cooking apples, peeled and sliced
> Sprinkle of semolina
> 25g sugar
> 1 tsp cinnamon
> Handful of blackberries or sultanas (optional)

1. Roll out half the pastry to form the base of your pie.
2. Line the base and cook blind for 10 minutes in a moderate oven.
3. Sprinkle the pastry base with semolina before adding the apple to avoid soggy bottoms!
4. Place the cooking apples on the pastry, sprinkle with sugar and cinnamon. (You can even add a handful of blackberries or sultanas to make it extra special!)
5. Cover with the remaining pastry.
6. Wet the top of your pie with a splash of milk or water, and sprinkle over it a light layer of sugar.

7. Bake in a moderate oven for 35 minutes until golden brown.

8. Serve with yoghurt, ice cream, crème fraîche or cream.

Healthy oat bars
Costs £1.20 for 10–12 bars

These are great fillers and healthy too. You are looking at £1.50 to buy a similar bar in a coffee shop so why not make your own? This recipe is very simple and a bit of a cheat!

> 175g butter
> 200g brown sugar
> 200g honey or golden syrup (if you have very sweet tooth)
> 500g value muesli
> 50g mixed fruit

1. Melt the butter and sugar in a saucepan over a gentle heat. Add the honey when the butter has dissolved.

2. Add the muesli and mixed fruit and stir well.

3. Pour into a lined baking tin, and press down with the back of a spoon to form a solid base.

4. Bake in a moderate oven for 15 minutes until golden.

5. Cut into slices when cool.

6. For extra decadence (if you aren't worried about waistlines), melt some plain chocolate and coat the slices.

Basic sponge

Costs less than £2 for one large cake or 12 muffins

Use this sponge recipe as a basis for other cakes. Muffins are very popular in coffee shops and cost a whopping £1.50–£2 each. You can make your own muffins with the following recipes – I have included my favourite variations.

> 225g self-raising flour
> 225g butter
> 225g sugar
> 4 eggs

1. In a bowl or mixer, cream the butter and sugar together until soft.

2. Beat the eggs and then add a little at a time. Mix well.

3. Sift the flour, add gently and fold in to the mixture.

4. When thoroughly mixed you can decide what you are going to make!

Sponge

If you're making a plain sponge, it is ready to bake. If you want to flavour the sponge, here are some suggestions.

Chocolate sponge cake

Add approximately 50g of cocoa but it must be sifted. If the mixture is too dry, add a touch of water. Place in two lined sponge tins. For a rich chocolate cake, add chopped dates and plain chocolate chips. Place in a lined tin.

Coffee cake

Mix 2–3 tsp of good quality instant coffee with a small

amount of hot water to dissolve the granules. Add this to the cake mix.

Lemon cake

Add the grated rind of one lemon, and 50ml of lemon juice. You can also mix in a small amount of lemon curd if you are feeling adventurous.

Apple cake

Add chopped cooking apples, 2 tsp of dried cinnamon and 50g of raisins or mixed fruit.

Baking

For all of these variations, place the mixture in a thoroughly lined cake tin. I always coat the tin with butter and then sprinkle with flour to ensure a good non-stick base, even when I'm using non-stick pans. Then bake at 180°C for 20–25 minutes until firm. To test that your cake is ready, insert a knife into the centre of the cake; if the knife comes out wet, it is not yet cooked. It should be firm to the touch and coming away slightly from the edges.

Muffins

Make the cake mix as above. Here are some varieties that work well, but feel free to experiment.

Triple chocolate muffins

Mix 30g of sifted cocoa powder into the cake mix. Add approximately 75g of chocolate chips (white, plain or milk, or a combination of all three).

Raspberry coconut and white chocolate muffins

Add 30g of desiccated coconut to the basic cake mix. Add a handful of frozen or fresh raspberries and a handful of white chocolate chips. Do not over stir.

Lemon curd muffins

Add the rind and juice of one lemon to the basic cake mix. Stir well. Half fill muffin cases with this mixture, then add a small teaspoon of lemon curd to each, finishing with a topping of cake mix. When the muffins are baked and while they're still hot, drizzle lemon juice over them and sprinkle with brown sugar.

Blueberry muffins

Add a handful of fresh or frozen blueberries to the basic cake mix.

Spicy muffins

Add 2 tsp of cinnamon, a sprinkle of nutmeg and ½ tsp of allspice to the basic cake mix. Add a generous handful of raisins or mixed dried fruit.

Baking

For all of these variations, place the mixture in lined muffin cases and bake in at 180°C for 15 minutes. I normally make two different flavours by dividing the cake mix into two bowls.

Simple no-bake lemon cheesecake
Costs £2.20 for eight servings

2 lemons
1 pot of cream cheese
1/2 packet of digestive biscuits, crumbed
50g butter
150ml thick double cream
1small pot of natural yoghurt
Plain chocolate

1. Melt the butter in a pan and add the biscuit crumbs.
2. Pack the biscuit mix into the bottom of a lined flan case.
3. Place in the fridge to cool.
4. Meanwhile, place the soft cheese into a bowl and add the rind and juice of two lemons. Add the cream and yoghurt and stir well.
5. Pour onto the biscuit base and leave to set.
Garnish with grated plain chocolate before serving.

Try adding variety by using different kinds of biscuits – a combination of ginger and digestive work well together.

Simple fruit crumble

Costs less than £2 for four servings
This is a very simple and very nutritious dish.

Stewed fruit of your choice – apples, apple and blackberry, apple and blackcurrant, plum and apple, rhubarb and strawberry, or whatever variety you can think of
Generous handful of value muesli
Generous handful of porridge oats
Generous handful of desiccated coconut
30g sugar
25g plain flour

1. Stew the fruit gently but not until completely soft.
In a bowl, mix the muesli, porridge oats and coconut together.
2. Add the sugar and plain flour and mix well.
3. Place the stewed fruit in an ovenproof dish. Cover evenly with the crumble mix.
4. Bake in a moderate oven for 20 minutes.

CHAPTER SIX

Beauty

'THOUGH WE TRAVEL THE WORLD OVER TO
FIND THE BEAUTIFUL, WE MUST CARRY IT
WITH US OR WE FIND IT NOT.'

Emerson

We all want to look good. Read any women's lifestyle magazine and you will be inundated with adverts, promotions and editorial, all promoting the next best beauty product designed to make our lives perfect, our skin glowing and to take literally years off us. The sad reality is we are more likely to lose money than gain eternal youth.

As a journalist, I have written many beauty features. There is more freedom within the journalist world now, but beauty editors are still under pressure to keep the key advertisers happy. When I was editor of a national magazine, I must admit I would give a better review to those companies who sent the best freebies. The moral of this is not to believe everything you read in a magazine. If you are looking for honest reviews, blogs are best. They have no advertisers to please and no freebies for bribery. Have a look at www.the-beauty-pages.com or www.beauty-blog.co.uk and I am sure you will soon find your own favourites.

The old adage 'You get what you pay for' does not always apply to beauty products. In 2008, a national paper surveyed anti-ageing creams. Top brands including L'Oreal, Olay and even the celebrities' choice Crème de la Mer competed against lesser-known economy ranges. The big surprise was that Aldi's anti-ageing cream at £1.89 won. This cream, voted Best Buy by a number of reviews and experts, reputedly leaves skin glowing, smoothes wrinkles and has a facial-like quality. You may also remember the buying frenzy for No7 anti-ageing products after an independent review voted it best product.

I have spoken to a number of skincare consultants

asking what they feel is the best product for the skin. As with journalists, a lot depends on what the consultant is selling in his or her clinic, but I have had some genuine advice.

Kirsti Schuba, managing director at Collin UK (the UK distributor of luxury French skincare house Collin Paris) says, 'The least expensive anti-ageing product is a good exfoliator. Exfoliators remove dead skin cells, thus allowing better penetration of ingredients from serums and creams. Exfoliation stimulates natural cellular regeneration, making the skin act in a more youthful way by renewing itself. The skin is radiant in good health, and is both supple and soft – quite literally making you more youthful inside and out. This goes for the face and body.'

Main Factors for Good Skin

The main factors for having good skin seem to be:

- Drinking plenty of water. This does seem to be the answer not just to health but also to good skin.
- Good genetics. If your parents and grandparents have good skin, the chances are you will too.
- Not smoking. Smoking not only causes more lines on the face but it depletes the body of antioxidants and vitamin C.
- Not drinking. Excessive alcohol consumption has a negative effect on the liver, which therefore has a negative effect on the skin.
- A healthy diet. I know it is boring for some but, really, you are what you eat and the best way to good skin is

to feed your body with good ingredients.

- Use a moisturiser with built-in sunscreen daily, even in the winter months. Choose a minimum of 15 SPF for the best protection.
- Exfoliate regularly. This rids the body of dead skin cells, but don't use harsh products as they can strip the natural oils from the skin.

Make-up Savvy

Boots ran a great advert in 2008, showing a girl buying make-up and discarding it in a skip overflowing with bad purchases. They were promoting their free DVD (a fantastic marketing campaign that ensured we all rushed out and bought the products featured in the DVD). We are all guilty of impulse make-up and beauty buys without knowing how to apply them or if they really suit us in the first place.

Make the most of the free advice and trials, but don't be swayed into buying something you don't want. Streamline your make-up. Look at your make-up bag – do you use it all? How old are some of the products? Declutter and start buying with savvy. Was the purple glitter eye shadow really a good buy? Do you really need 12 lipsticks? Get to know what works best for you and stick with them.

Fashionista not fashion slave

We all love to follow fashion trends but learn what suits you and what doesn't. If you want to go for fashion, be aware that it will only have a short life – so if you really want that purple eye shadow, it should be a budget buy not a designer one. Think logically about the use of your product. Are you going to use it again? Will it suit you? If you are in doubt, walk away. If you love it, try to find the same item cheaper elsewhere.

Mineral make-up

I spent years trying to work out which is the best make-up for my skin. I am pale with auburn/brunette hair. Foundation always looked heavy and never suited my skin tone. I could never achieve that natural look. I then discovered mineral make-up and to be honest, I would never use anything else. It does not clog my skin and I don't have the telltale tidemark or unnatural tinge to my skin. I use Susan Posnick Colorflo but have tried a variety of brands and all have been good value for money. Mineral make-up lasts a long time so it is a good investment. Most brands now have a mineral make-up range, so there should be something out there to suit your budget and you skin type.

Mineral make-up is free from dyes, preservatives, wax and perfumes so can be used on sensitive skin.

Budget make-up

There is nothing wrong with buying budget make-up if you like it and if it suits your needs. As with most things in life, some products are better than others, so buy wisely – just because something is cheap does not make it a bargain. Lipstick is a point in case. I have found budget lipsticks wear off very quickly, whereas the colour-stay formulas really do last. If you don't want to go to the expense of a long lasting lipstick, then go back in time and buy Lipcote for £3.49. Suddenly your 99p lipstick will transform into staying put for up to eight hours and Lipcote is still half the price of the leading brands (such as L'Oreal Infallible Lipstick Duo priced at over £10).

I love Elf (www.eyeslipsface.co.uk) where most products are a mere £1.50. If you sign up to the newsletter, you can get additional bargains and sale alerts. George of Asda, Barbara Daly at Tesco, W7 at Peacocks and 2True from Superdrug are all budget brands with their finger on the pulse of current trends.

The latest must-have

You can't read a woman's magazine without stumbling upon the latest must-have or celebrity choice make-up. As we discussed earlier, you have to take some of the advice from beauty editors with a pinch of salt, however, if the product is also appearing on blogs and your best friend swears by it, well, there may be an element of truth. One product to make a big splash recently is Yves Saint Laurent Touche Éclat (winner of the Instyle Beauty Award for best under-eye concealer 2008 and 2009). At £22, it would seem to be a luxury buy, but it does last and the results are worth the added luxury. Remember, if you have streamlined your make-up bag and cut down on your unnecessary make-up purchases, you can now afford to buy make-up that works for you.

There are a number of great websites where you can get some lovely bargains and discounts off popular and designer brands:

- www.feelunique.com
- www.HQoutletstore.com
- www.shoprush.co.uk
- www.besthairbrands.com
- www.cyvilianhairstore.co.uk
- www.halfpriceperfumes.co.uk
- www.buycosmetics.com

Forum for free

If you are able to get online, have a look at some forums. There are many beauty forums all giving great advice. You can also look at the money-saving sites that will highlight any special offers, freebies and deals.

Magazine appeal

Keep an eye on magazine offers and cover mounts. They often give away products that are worth far more than the price of the magazine.

Free gifts

Companies often offer free gifts to entice new buyers. Boots is great with many offers and, if you have an Advantage card, you will get discounts, money-saving coupons and even free gifts. Make sure you use the machine in store to get the best deals.

Professional Pampering

There are times in a girl's life when only a professional pampering session will do – if only it was not so expensive. Yet pampering can still be possible if you use some savvy thinking.

Girls' night in

Why not hire a therapist or hairdresser for the night? Get your friends together to share the expense and share a great evening together being pampered. This is a wonderful alternative to a girly night out.

The apprentice

Trainees are a great way of getting a budget hairdo or a pampering session. It is not as scary as it sounds. All apprentices are accompanied by trained professionals, so you really are in safe hands. Salons are often asking for models and your local college will offer dramatically discounted pampering for everyone. I have had some amazing hairdos at my local college. The trainees are often keen to make their mark and, unlike some hairdressers, seem to listen to what you want. Be prepared to spend a little while longer for your session, but you are still looked after with cups of tea and some great chats.

Big names versus word of mouth

As with most things in life, you pay more for the brand. Well known hairdressers and beauty salons do come with a higher price tag, but you don't always get what you pay for. Word of mouth is the best recommendation. If a friend or colleague has a great hairdo, fake tan or manicure, ask them for the salon's name and number. They will be incredibly flattered and you will hopefully gain a great contact.

Change your look for less

You can change your look with a few simple accessories. Hairpieces cost as little as £10 and look great for a fun change of style. Hothair (www.hothair.co.uk) sell fringe pieces that simply clip into your hair ready for a change of appearance. High street retailers such as Superdrug and Accessorize offer some great inexpensive products, perfect for a night out.

Learn to budget and bargain

If you really don't want to give up on your luxury pampering, just learn to budget or bargain. Whenever I want something that is not strictly within my normal budgets, I try to create the money by taking on extra work, selling something or, if all else fails, saving up. It is amazing what a bit of motivation can do. I fell in love with a pair of boots last winter. They were not obscenely expensive but expensive enough for me to have to think hard before purchasing. I decided to have a hunt through my wardrobe and found quite a few clothes and shoes I no longer wanted. After five days on eBay, I had raised nearly double the amount I needed for the boots.

Thinking before you spend gives you that all-important pause before purchasing. Analyse your motives for buying. Do you need it? Will you use it? Can you buy it cheaper elsewhere? Most importantly, can you afford it? Only buy when you are sure you can answer all these questions honestly.

Create your own spa

It would be nice to spend a few days away in a luxury spa

but, sadly, life is not like that. Try to capture some 'you' time and learn to unwind. Nicola Brookes, Spa Guru, gives her low-cost, no-fuss tips on how to create your own home spa and detox without spending a fortune.

Get in the mood...
Make sure the space around you is clean and comfortable, so you won't be distracted by anything or anyone. Switch off your mobile phone, turn down any harsh lights and light some candles to create a peaceful, tranquil atmosphere – ready for relaxation.

Aromatherapy your room...
Bring a sense of relaxation to your home by burning some beautifully scented aromatherapy oil. Lavender, juniper and rose are particularly good for relieving stress.

Scrub away...
Raid the kitchen cupboards to slough off dull winter skin with an exfoliating scrub. Mix a handful of oatmeal with some almond or olive oil. Apply to the skin in circular motions, getting rid of any dead skin, and then shower off.

Have a soothing bath...
Epsom salts cost a fraction of the price of designer bath oil and can be picked up at your local chemist. Add two cups to your bath to soothe sore muscles and help flush toxins from the skin.

Get steamy...
You could pay hundreds of pounds for a salon facial – why, when a bowl of water is all that's required to open

your pores? Pour some hot (not boiling) water into a large bowl, add some chamomile teabags and sit for five minutes with a towel over your head to get a healthy glow.

Indulge in a massage…
Massage is one of the most pleasant ways to help you relax and it's free! Persuade a friend or a partner to pamper you, using your favourite body moisturiser or by simply using a few drops of olive oil.

Meditate…
Try candle meditation to swiftly detox your emotions and find emotional balance. Spend a few minutes looking at the flame of a candle, placed at eye level, and then close your eyes for ten minutes, clearing your mind of any thoughts.

Natural Skincare and Beauty

Making your own skincare products is not only cheaper, it is also safe, healthy and natural. There are a huge amount of chemicals within our skincare. Some of these chemicals are known carcinogens, others are known to irritate the skin, cause allergic reactions and even premature ageing – not great for products that are supposed to keep you looking young and healthy! A huge amount of chemicals are derived from petroleum. For example, isopropyl SD-40 is a solvent, polyethylene glycol is found in oven cleaners, propylene glycol is found in automatic brake fluid and antifreeze. Add to this over 4,000 synthetic fragrances, parabens and sodium lauryl sulphate and it is easy to see why natural products are becoming more popular.

Making your own skincare products does not involve any special equipment, a laboratory or a degree in chemistry. The recipes below are simple to follow and include ingredients found in your home. These recipes really are good enough to eat! They are free from preservatives and chemicals so they have to be refrigerated and used within three to seven days unless stated otherwise.

There are also skincare workshops all over the country. My favourite is Careys Manor & Senspa at £25 per person including smoothie, all ingredients and use of facilities: www.senspa.co.uk

The face
Strawberry and banana cream cleanser
    1 tsp plain yoghurt
    1 tsp unwhipped double cream
    1 tsp mashed banana
    1 tsp mashed strawberry

Mix all ingredients together in a bowl. Apply to the face and neck. Gently massage and remove with warm water.

Yoghurt and honey cleanser
    ½ tbsp honey
    2 tsp natural yoghurt
    ½ tsp rose water

Combine all ingredients in a bowl. Apply to the face and neck, gently massaging into skin. Remove with warm water.

Avocado cleanser

    1 egg yoke
    1 tsp milk
    1 tbsp mashed avocado

Combine the ingredients and beat until you have a thin creamy consistency. Apply to the face and neck and massage into the skin. Remove with warm water.

Green tea and aloe vera toner

    2 organic green tea teabags
    100ml pure aloe vera
    1 tsp manuka honey
    150ml boiling water

Add boiling water to the teabags. Add honey and leave to cool. When cool, add the aloe vera and then bottle ready for use. Soak a cotton wool pad and wipe all over the face after cleansing. Keep refrigerated and use within one month.

Aloe vera and rose water toner

    200ml rose water
    200ml pure aloe vera

Combine the liquids in a bottle and shake well. Soak a cotton wool pad and wipe all over the face after cleansing. Keep refrigerated and use within two months.

Cucumber and witch hazel toner

    ½ a skinless cucumber
    100ml witch hazel

Add both ingredients to a blender and whizz until combined. Soak a cotton wool pad and wipe all over the face after cleansing.

Soothing calendula and chamomile cream

    150ml boiling water

    100ml extra virgin olive oil or omega rich oil

    2 organic chamomile teabags

    1 tbsp manuka honey

    2 tsp vegetable glycerine

    1 tsp beeswax

    3 drops chamomile essential oil

    3 drops calendula essential oil

Add boiling water to the chamomile teabags and allow to cool. Place a glass bowl on top of the saucepan of boiling water. Add the oil, honey and beeswax to the bowl. Slowly add glycerine. Stir continuously until all ingredients are dissolved and combined. Remove from the heat. Add the chamomile tea and essential oils to the melted beeswax formula, stirring all the time. Keep refrigerated and use within two months.

Almond facial scrub

    1 tsp honey

    ½ tsp plain yoghurt

    ¼ tsp rose water

    1 tbsp ground almonds

Mix the ingredients together in bowl. Apply to cleansed skin. Massage over face and neck using small circular movements. Rinse with warm water.

Banana facial scrub

　　1 tsp ground rice
　　1 tsp salt
　　1 tsp coconut oil
　　1 tsp mashed banana
　　½ tsp lemon juice

Combine the ingredients in a bowl. Apply to cleansed skin. Massage over face and neck. Rinse off with warm water.

Rejuvenating and firming facial mask

　　1 tsp egg white
　　½ tsp orange juice
　　¼ tsp lemon juice
　　1 tsp honey
　　2 tbsp oatmeal

Lightly beat the egg white. Mix with all other ingredients. Apply to cleansed face and neck. Leave for 10 to 15 minutes. Rinse off with warm water and moisturise as normal.

Balancing mud facial mask

　　½ tbsp rhassoul mud
　　1 tsp honey
　　½ tsp lemon juice
　　¼ tsp witch hazel
　　2 drops jojoba oil

Mix the ingredients together in a bowl. Apply to cleansed face and neck. Leave for 10 to 15 minutes. Rinse off with warm water and moisturise as normal.

Moisturising avocado facial mask

1 tbsp mashed avocado

1 tsp honey

½ tsp lemon juice

1 pinch spirulina powder (optional)

Mix the ingredients together in a bowl. Apply to cleansed face and neck. Leave for 10 to 15 minutes. Rinse off with warm water and moisturise as normal.

Apricot and avocado moisturising facial mask

2 tbsp mashed avocado

2 tbsp mashed apricot

Combine the ingredients in a bowl. Apply to cleansed face and neck. Leave for 10 to 15 minutes. Rinse off with warm water and moisturise as normal.

Kiwi and papaya rejuvenating facial mask

2 tbsp mashed kiwi

2 tbsp mashed papaya

1 tbsp ground rice

Combine the ingredients in a bowl. Apply to cleansed face and neck. Leave for 10 to 15 minutes. Rinse off with warm water and moisturise as normal.

The body

Rice and yoghurt body scrub

2 tbsp ground rice

1 tbsp natural yoghurt

4 tsp rose water

Mix the ingredients together in a bowl. Massage over the whole body and rinse off with water.

Rose geranium bath bomb

- 2–3 tsp rose petals
- 1 tbsp citric acid powder
- 3 tbsp bicarbonate of soda
- 10–15 drops of rose geranium essential oil
- 1 tsp grapeseed oil

Mix the citric acid and bicarbonate of soda together. Add the remaining ingredients and mix well. Place in a pastry cutter and press down very firmly to form a solid base. Leave to set for at least one to two hours until dry and hard. Store in foil to keep moisture out. When ready to use, simply drop into the bath to create a mini explosion. It will keep for months if stored correctly.

Lavender relaxation bath salts

- 100g dried lavender
- 200g Epsom salts
- 100g oatmeal
- 100g salt
- 100g bicarbonate of soda

Combine the ingredients and store in a jar until needed. Add a generous handful whilst running the bath. Lie back and relax.

Kiwi, papaya and honey body scrub

- 100g coarse crystal or sea salt
- 2 tbsp mashed kiwi
- 2 tbsp mashed papaya
- 2 tsp manuka honey
- 100g natural yoghurt
- 2 tsp sweet almond oil

Combine all ingredients in a bowl. Apply to the body and leave for 15 minutes. Rinse well.

Ginger, lavender and rose body scrub

> 200g coarse crystal or sea salt
> 100g lavender flowers
> 100g rose petals
> 400ml sweet almond oil
> 25 drops ginger essential oil
> 20 drops rose geranium essential oil
> 20 drops lavender essential oil

Combine the dry ingredients and place into a jar. In a jug combine the almond oil with the essential oils and pour into the jar of salt. Use as a body scrub when required.

Fragrant soap

> 1 bar pure unperfumed soap, grated
> 500ml rose water
> 500ml glycerine
> 50 drops of your favourite essential oil
> 2 tbsp rose petals

Using a glass bowl over a saucepan of boiling water, add the rose water, glycerine and grated soap to the bowl. Stir until melted and then remove from the heat. Add the essential oils and petals and stir well. Place into moulds or pour into a small baking tin (lined with cling-film). The soap will take at least two days to set, then cut it into bars and use. You can buy silicon soap moulds (www.baldwins.co.uk) if you want a professional finish.

Exfoliating soap

  1 bar pure unperfumed soap, grated

  500ml rose water

  500ml glycerine

  4 tbsp coarse oatmeal

  25 drops lemon essential oil

  25 drops tea tree essential oil

Using a glass bowl over a saucepan of boiling water, add the rose water, glycerine and grated soap to the bowl. Stir until melted and then remove from heat. Add the essential oils and oatmeal and stir well. Place into moulds or pour into a small baking tin (lined with cling-film). The soap will take at least two days to set. This is great for cleaning dirty hands – particularly after gardening!

Hands

Lemon and sugar hand scrub

  2 tbsp sugar

  20ml lemon juice

Combine the ingredients and use immediately. Great for softening hands and gets rid of nasty odours.

Rose hand lotion

  40ml rose water

  30 drops rose geranium essential oil

  1 tsp honey

  ¼ tsp distilled vinegar

  2 tsp vegetable glycerine

Combine all ingredients together and place in a glass bottle. Shake well before each use.

Rich hand cream
   2 tsp evening primrose oil
   2 tsp sweet almond oil
   10 drops lemon oil
   5 drops geranium essential oil
   5 drops lavender essential oil

Combine ingredients and place in a dark glass bottle. Store in a cool place and use to soften hands (or feet) when needed.

Spot busters

You don't have to be a teenager to suffer from the periodic outbreak of spots. I am in my late thirties and seem to be going through a pre-menstrual spotty stage. Like clockwork, one or two spots will appear a week prior to my period. The telltale signs are itchy skin, inflammation and finally the eruption – yuk!

Most creams and lotions available on the market contain harsh stripping agents. Yes they do remove the grease and grime from your skin, but they also remove the natural oils. The result? Your skin tries to compensate for the lack of natural oils by producing more oils.

Having tried many wonder creams, I have finally found a cheap and effective solution to the occasional outbreak of spots. Many of my friends, including me, use toothpaste. At night, dab a blob on the offending spot and, by morning, it will have dried out significantly.

Aspirin is another great zit-zapper. Mix uncoated aspirins with water to form a paste. Dab onto the spot to help dry them out. For those more adventurous types, you can make a face pack and apply once a week.

Blackheads can be removed by mixing bicarbonate of soda with water. Apply to problem areas and leave for five minutes before rinsing with warm water.

Women's issues...

If you're a man reading this, you might want to skip this section. I am talking about periods. Sanitary towels and tampons are expensive. I was once sent a Mooncup to review for an article I was writing. I must say that I would never have thought about buying such a device. However, one day, inevitably, my period arrived unannounced and, unprepared, I opted to use my freebie. I won't go into personal details, but hasten to add that since this day I have not used anything else.

For me it is preferable to any other form of sanitary protection. It is better for the environment, better for my health (no more risk of toxic shock syndrome or irritation from sanitary towels) and it has saved me money. There are two types available: the Mooncup for £19.99 (www.mooncup.co.uk) and Femmecup for £14.99 (www.femmecup.com). Both look pretty much the same. They are available from Boots or health food shops.

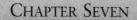

CHAPTER SEVEN

Clothing

'FASHION IS GENERAL.
STYLE IS INDIVIDUAL.'
Edna Woolman Chase

Clothing is a very personal choice. People buy for a multitude of reasons. Some buy to suit their body shape, others must have the latest trend. Some buy classic and others would only ever wear designer. One thing they all have in common, they all shop to suit their budget.

Budget Clothing

When I started investigating how to save money on clothing, I came up against quite heated debates on the pros and cons of budget clothing. I know the ethical arguments for budget clothing and I agree with them, but I have also been in the position in my life where I could not afford anything but budget clothes. It is disheartening enough to know you are unable to afford the clothes you would love, without some know-it-all writer making you feel worse. Ask shoppers where they would shop if they had millions of pounds, I doubt they would choose Primark but, for those with very little money, Primark and its contemporaries help to give a taste of the latest fashion without the hefty price tag.

I recently wrote an article on high street budget chic, with some great results. TK Maxx, Matalan, Peacocks (which is great for shoes!), George at Asda, Tesco's Florence and Fred, Sainsbury's Tu and Primark all offer their take on designer trends. The secret with budget clothing is to mix and match with some vintage and designer pieces – do not dress head to toe in budget or it will scream cheap.

Avoiding the landfill

According to Defra, almost 74% of the two million tonnes of clothes bought in the UK each year end up in landfills. Environmentalists blame the cheap, high street clothing market for encouraging this throw-away culture, but I can't help feeling that the government should also take some of the blame and more funding should be available to investigate different ways of recycling. Surely there is are better ways to reuse and recycle unwanted garments to avoid this kind of quantity being discarded.

Yes, in an ideal world we would buy garments that were well made and that would last for years, but we need companies to help us find these when living on a tight budget. I read one article from a journalist who was obviously paid more than me. She recommended buying a £350 Diane von Furstenberg wrap dress instead of a high street alternative. I totally understand where she was coming from and, yes, it would look better and last, but in reality would you spend £350 on a dress if you were on a limited income? That amount could buy me a winter's worth of heating or a quarter of electricity – not as nice as the dress admittedly, but the oil will probably keep me a lot warmer.

One way to stop your clothes prematurely landing on the landfill is to look after your clothing. Even budget clothing can look better if you look after it well. My mum used to despair with me. I hated ironing my clothes and never really took that much care – my response had always been life was too short to iron. I was wrong. My mum looks after her clothes, starches where she should, and irons and hangs them correctly. Her reward for this dedication is to have clothes that last well and look good. It seems that a little investment and time can reap huge rewards.

Shoes also warrant a bit of care and attention. Polish regularly and use your local cobbler to repair the heels. Stuff your boots with rolled up newspaper to keep them in tiptop condition.

If you are concerned about landfill, why not sell your unwanted items or even offer them on Freecycle or to a charity shop. If they are beyond help, use them for rags for cleaning or dusting. Marks & Spencer have teamed up with Oxfam and have created what they call their wardrobe intervention. Customers can get a £5 voucher if they sign up and take their unwanted Marks & Spencer's clothes to Oxfam. The £5 voucher can be used with any purchase over £35.

Key ways to contribute to the reduction of clothing on landfill sites include:

- Avoid impulse buys and obscure fashion trends. They are short lived and will often end up being thrown out after limited use.
- Buy the best quality clothes you can afford as they will last longer.
- Look after your clothes to keep them in pristine condition.
- Reduce, reuse, recycle. Think of ways to get the most out of your clothing – adapting and reusing.
- Sell unwanted clothes to earn yourself some extra money.
- Give unwanted clothes away to charity shops or Freecycle, or hold clothing swap parties with friends.

The ethics of budget clothing

Child labour is unacceptable in our world today. There is no excuse for why companies employ in this way. However, this practice is not exclusive to budget ranges – there have been recorded cases of some designer and premium brands using child labour in some of its factories. If you are concerned, ask the question and do your research. Some high street companies promote their ethical policy, such as Marks & Spencer. Others will try to hide their practices. It is up to you, the consumer, to make the decision that suits your ethics and your budget.

Have a look at some of the following excellent websites for ethical fashion inspiration:

- www.peopletree.com
- www.nomadsclothing.com
- www.green-uk.com
- www.adili.com
- www.devidoll.com
- www.Bochica.co.uk
- www.deployworkshop.com
- www.greenrewards.co.uk

Clothing swap parties

This is nothing dodgy! Clothing swap parties are great fun – a good excuse to get your friends together and share a bottle of wine while passing on some style tips. According to statistics, we only wear about a third of our wardrobe, so the occasional de-clutter should uncover some great finds. I have skirts purchased over three years ago I still have not worn, and to be honest I doubt I ever will. I still have my clothes from before my son was born

– in the days when I really was a size ten though of course did not appreciate it at the time. I really should part company with them now.

The key to holding a clothing swap party is to make sure you invite like-minded and similar sized friends to the party. It is not going to be any good for you if all your friends are a size eight and you are a size 14 – this is guaranteed to make you feel inadequate! Make a list of your friends' sizes and ensure there are at least two people to each size. Friends should bring at least five items, but not underwear. Make sure the clothes are clean, ironed and hung on hangers. Shoes should also be clean and polished. You don't want to feel like you are at a jumble sale – more an exclusive members only club! Have a plan in case two people want the same item – perhaps a fashion parade where other guests vote for the best look, or simply toss a coin.

This type of party also works well with other items, such as nursery items, toys, music and even DVDs.

Sign up for the best deals

Many retailers offer a membership or newsletter you can sign up to for free. The advantage of this is access to some great offers and discounts. Check online with your favourite retailer, beauty manufacturer or high street store. For example, at the time of writing Wallis are offering 10% discount for those who sign up to their newsletter. Bonmarch Bonus Club and WHSmith Privilege Club offer regular discounts and savings.

Designer for Less

If you love designer clothing but don't have the budget, use a bit of savvy and you can find some great bargains. The internet makes life so much easier. All designer stores have sales, so ask when they start and put it in your diary. America started the secret sale, and thankfully it has now reached the UK, but only in the bigger cities. Members are emailed or texted about designer sales (usually at least 50% reductions). These sales take place at a chosen venue and last only a matter of hours.

For more designer fixes, there are some great sites that offer current and last season's ranges at discounted prices. Have a look at:

• www.mandmdirect.com
• www.bargainista.co.uk
• www.brandalley.co.uk

EBay is a great site for clothing but, beware, there are a lot of fake goods out there, particularly when dealing with designer labels.

Used not abused

Findings from a survey by www.Bigwardrobe.com found that women in the UK spend a staggering £6 billion every year on clothes, shoes and accessories they'll never wear. Used and unwanted clothing offers a great way for the savvy thinker to save money but retain that all important style. Find bargains at boot sales, tabletop sales, charity shops, markets and online. You may also have a clothing exchange shop near you, where the retailer takes a percentage of the sale from your unwanted items.

Online, you can look at the old favourite eBay, but there is a huge number of clothing sites dedicated to finding new homes for unwanted items. There has also been an increase in clothing swap sites. Here are some of my favourites:

- www.bigwardrobe.com
- www.buymywardrobe.com
- www.lovemissdaisy.com
- www.fashionexchange.co.uk

Vintage Style

The joy of vintage is never seeing someone else wearing the same item. You can create your own unique style mixing the old with the new, and the designer with the high street. Boot sales, junk shops and charity shops can all have some fantastic hidden treasures. The internet is great but, a word of warning, vintage sizing may vary from today's sizing, so be prepared. If in doubt, ask the seller to measure the garment for you.

Some of my favourite sites include:

- www.veryvintageclothing.co.uk
- www.myvintage.co.uk
- www.candysays.co.uk
- www.marthascloset.co.uk
- www.vintageveronica.co.uk
- www.devotedtovintage.co.uk

Love the Skin You're In

Many of us, especially women, feel inadequate and find fault with our own bodies. We may not know how to make the best of our assets and so spend a lot of money and time buying the wrong things. I am a prime example. I have large boobs, a bit of a tummy and narrow hips … a nightmare to dress. My boob size means buying large tops but, with a smaller frame, they hang off my shoulders and gape around the neck. Dresses are a complete no no, unless I want to walk around in a tent. I used to feel upset, inadequate, dowdy and undesirable and my poor husband took the brunt of my frustration.

My mum gave me a Trinny and Susannah book. Now, love them or hate them, they do give good advice for certain body shapes. I am still not satisfied with my body shape but at least I am a step closer in knowing how to make the best of the situation. There are other books and advisers out there so, if in doubt, find out which are the best clothes for your body shape. When in a shop ask the assistant for advice (unless they are the sulky teenager variety!). Find someone you admire who has a similar body shape to yours and try to emulate how they dress.

It does not matter what size or shape you are, it is the way you carry yourself and the confidence you exude that gives off that irresistible message.

You're Hired

It is not as stupid as it sounds. Hiring items is a great way to saving money, as long as you do your figures correctly. If you are attending a special function and need a designer handbag, it is worth paying a hire charge for a fraction of the cost of buying the real thing. However if you intend to keep hiring this bag, you will end up paying more than the bag is worth, so think savvy.

Here are some great sites:
- www.fashionhire.co.uk
- www.handbaghirehq.co.uk
- www.RentYourRocks.com

Designer glasses for less

Glasses can cost a fortune, particularly if you prefer designer frames. There are two great websites offering great deals and savings. www.glassesdirect.co.uk is the largest online seller of prescription glasses. Prices start at £19 for own-brands leading up to designer frames from the likes of Vera Wang and Nicole Farhi. I also like www.wantglasses.co.uk with prices starting from £15.

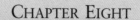

CHAPTER EIGHT

Raising the Family

'ALWAYS BE NICE TO YOUR CHILDREN
BECAUSE THEY ARE THE ONES WHO WILL
CHOOSE YOUR REST HOME.'
Phyllis Diller

There is no doubt that raising a family is expensive. I think our expectations of creating that perfect childhood have become embroiled with a need to give our children more and more material possessions, but we have neglected to give them the freedom and innocence of a real childhood. Janey Lee Grace (author of *Imperfectly Natural Woman*, *Imperfectly Natural Baby and Toddler* and *Imperfectly Natural Home*) has worked with me on this chapter. Here she discusses some great approaches to the early years of parenthood.

The Formative Years

Kids are expensive there's no doubt, but it's perfectly possible to have fun without spending too much money. Think back to your own childhood and I can guarantee your favourite memories will be of long days playing outside, running on a windswept beach, climbing trees, paddling in streams and picking blackberries.

Somehow along the way, 'progress' has brought us an industry based around 'bringing up children'. We're expected as 'good parents' to provide all the latest toys and gadgets, a wide range of entertainment from baby French classes to Toddler Tumbling sessions, plus exclusive foreign holidays with clubs where children can be out of our sight most of the day. The scary thing is that we are raising a nation of children who are never allowed to play unsupervised or experience the joys of being outside in nature. There is a temptation to over-complicate, overspend and fill up our days with playdates, extra tuition and a whole range of activities for even our tiny babies and toddlers, when actually we should be simply getting on with the business of living.

I confess to being a fan of 'attachment parenting'. It sounds new and trendy but it's actually rather old-fashioned, eschewing the need to possess all the latest gadgets, toys and designer label clothes. It incorporates breastfeeding, baby wearing, safe co-sleeping and positive discipline. It is about being 'attached', that is avoiding long periods of separation between the parent and the child. Perhaps it should be called 'conscious parenting', because it's also about letting go and allowing your child to grow.

Jean Liedloff in The Continuum Concept says:

It would help immeasurably if we could see baby care as a non-activity. We should learn to regard it as nothing to do. Working, shopping, cooking, cleaning, walking and talking with friends are things to do, to make time for, to think of as activities. The baby (with other children) is simply brought along as a matter of course, no special time need be set aside for him apart from the minutes devoted to changing his nappies. His bath can be part of his mother's. Breastfeeding need not stop all other activity either. It's only a matter of changing one's baby-centred thought patterns to those more suitable for a capable, intelligent being whose nature it is to enjoy work and the companionship of other adults.

Apart from those wonderful few weeks of 'babymoon' when you really are in recovery and bonding mode, life should go on as normal and the baby should just fit in. If they are treated with respect as little human beings, they will respond beautifully to watching and 'helping' as you go about your daily work.

You don't need all the plans, arrangements, paraphernalia and worries that can come with trying to make your life more choreographed. Just give your baby their own space, let them discover, amuse and create in their own new world. Remember simple is good and let them become a part of their new family interacting in a natural way. Be a relaxed parent!

Enjoy your children

Children can be annoying, frustrating, unpredictable, uncompromising and totally exhausting. But boring – they are not. Children live in the 'now' and they are incredibly inventive and enthusiastic. If plonked in front of a TV screen while you get on with your business for hours on end they will become dullards and probably get cabin fever and play up. But when you connect with a child – even finding, dare I say it without sounding too cosmic, your own 'inner child' – it can all change in an instant.

You'll find that time is really all they want from you. One on one. A game of 'peep bo' is worth a million dollars to them, and they would (if they could) happily trade half an hour of your time for all the expensive toys in the world. They thrive on continual interaction. Include them in your group and family conversations. Even at two years old they understand more than you think!

Go for nature walks and don't be afraid to wear your own wellies and splash with them, pick wild flowers and study insects, you'll be amazed at how the world looks through a child's eyes if you take the time to really look.

Alternatives to buying more 'stuff'

When they're a little older and want 'stuff', make good use of local charity shops and car boot sales. Freecycle is also brilliant for outgrown kids' bikes, scooters and much loved toys that are still in perfectly serviceable condition. Put out a wanted message for what your child would like. Over the years I've been the recipient of a climbing frame, a sandpit and a child's motorbike. Make sure you reciprocate and put your own giveaways on there too.

Of course the library is a wonderful resource for children's books but there are also toy libraries in many towns that work on the same principle: you can borrow a toy (large or small) for a few weeks. Often children are starting to get bored after that period of time anyway. You could also organise a kids swap party. Get each family to bring a couple of toys or games they no longer want and then negotiate a swap. While you're at it, perhaps you could swap clothing too.

If you have a garden, you could build a mini activity course – sounds scary, but it can be as simple as planks raised just slightly off the ground and some log pieces for 'building'.

On rainy days, kids love messy play in the form of cooking or arts and crafts. You can make playdough using flour, salt, water and cream of tartar. Dye the playdough using spices or natural dyes (you can buy vegetable-based food colouring). Don't forget to have a look around when you're out and about for twigs, leaves, pine cones, etc, all of which can be used. A simple weaving activity for young children is to make a cross with twigs and then weave yarn or fabric over and under the twigs.

Rifle through charity shops to pick up buttons and collect other bits and pieces to make collages with. Simple bracelets and necklaces can also be made with buttons or painted pasta shells threaded onto cord or elastic.

It is really worth checking if there is a Scrap Store near to you. It is a very cheap source of all kinds of bits and pieces that can be used for collages, model making and costumes, such as offcuts of cellophane, paper or card. Mostly it's industry surplus so you are saving things from landfill. There is even an online version at www.uniquesocialenterprise.com

Old jumpers can be felted and cut up to make finger puppets, purses, etc. (Check that the jumper is wool.) You can make your own printing stamps from potatoes and also experiment with printing with various textured materials, such as bark, bubble wrap or scrunched-up paper.

Gardening

You probably realise I'm a big fan of kids being outdoors in practically all weathers. Children need to be outdoors for long stretches at a time and gardening is a fantastic way of getting exercise. It also gets them in tune with nature, helps them to think creatively, appreciate the environment and of course there's a wealth of educational opportunities ranging from biology, science and geography to even a bit of archaeology if you're lucky!

Of course, with children it has to be relatively instant so you will need a low maintenance area ready for the kids to claim as their patch. Herbs are fantastic and can be grown just in pots on the windowsill if you don't have a garden. Everyone can grow some mustard and sprouted seeds and children will also eat healthy food if they've grown and picked it themselves.

If you want inspiration to really get into gardening with your children The National Trust run family gardening days at many of their homes and gardens. See their website: www.nationaltrust.org.uk

It is hard to beat the Kitchen Garden Project in West London. Their regular open days attract thousands of visitors and along with complete tours of the gardens you can pick the herbs and even take some home with instructions for baking herby bread. There is also a working beehive and you can offer as a family to drop in and do the gardening: www.kitchengarden.org.uk

There is also the excellent Plant for Life initiative, which aims to encourage children to interact with nature and get their hands dirty. Find out more at: www.plantforlife.info

If all you are cultivating right now is couch potatoes and you are still not convinced, I highly recommend reading *Saving Our Children from Nature-Deficit Disorder* by Richard Louv.

Days out

It's amazing fun just to stroll through the park in all weathers with toddlers, such is their wonder at the slightest twig and soggy leaf, but if you want to head off on a day trip make sure you have a family railcard which will save a small fortune and look out for special offers on tickets. Usually if you join up with local families and go in as a group, you'll get a big discount even at popular attractions. If you need to stay overnight then don't forget the good old youth hostel. YHA has had a major revamp recently and, once you've bought your family membership, it's very cheap to stay. You can get family rooms and, no, you don't need to do the washing up.

A great educational but fun day out learning about the environment can be had at the Centre for Alternative Technology in Wales: www.cat.org.uk You can also volunteer to work there for a while and stay in one of their eco-cabins.

If you're lucky enough to get to Cornwall's the Eden Project, it has amazing things going on all year round for children including an ice rink in the winter months.

In Hertfordshire there is a wonderfully reconstructed Iron Age farmstead/encampment, Celtic Harmony. We were asked to bring a totally 'compostable after use' packed lunch and we came up with the idea of huge lettuce leaves tied around sandwiches! The kids had their faces 'daubed', made some incredible clay pendants and played Iron Age musical instruments. See www.celticharmony.org

City breaks are fantastic for kids. It is not just

London that offers excellence in museums and tourism for children and there are lots of ideas for holidays, activities, camps and more at www.eparenting.co.uk For specifically sustainable activities, subscribe to *The Green Parent* magazine (www.greenparent.co.uk) and look at www.naturalmatters.net

I'm sure you know this already, but it's your time that children really need. Whatever you do just find a way of switching off from everything else, even if only for a short while, and devote sole time to being with your children. That's what having fun as a family is really about. Remember how quickly the early years pass!

Adapted from Imperfectly Natural Baby and Toddler *(London: Orion Books). Janey Lee Grace is an author and owner of www.imperfectlynatural.com which has a thriving parenting forum.*

Watch Them Grow

I love the advice from Janey, but do not discount it as your child grows. Teenagers love impromptu childish games and frolics as much as a young child. There's nothing like watching my six-foot-tall son playing and laughing with his little brother. He is 18 this year but that will not stop him expecting a Christmas stocking, Easter egg hunt or wanting to eat the same 'kid style' treats as his little brother.

Kids grow so quickly. We need to enjoy every second and share the journey with them. Often we are so caught up in our own lives we forget they need and want to be with us. We don't want to look back at their childhood in years to come and wish we were more involved. Parenting is a gift and every day we should be thankful.

Music masters

Some parents dread their children coming home from school clutching the newsletter offering music lessons. They are often viewed as expensive, especially if once you have purchased the latest instrument, books and case the little darlings decide that they are no longer interested. We should all encourage our kids to be as creative as possible. The good news is I have found an excellent website where you can buy new instruments at a fraction of the price. www.karacha.com has some great deals, including maple violins and cases for less than £30.

If this is still out of your price range you could put an appeal out on Freecycle (www.freecycle.org) or scour your local paper, eBay or Gumtree. Speak to your school to see if there is any help, concessions or second-hand instruments for sale. They will also tell you of reputable music teachers in your area.

The modern world

As your children age, it becomes harder to keep them away from the perils of the modern world. Today computers are a fact of our lives and the social life for many. Social sites such as MySpace, Facebook, Bebo and Twitter are very popular. MSN Messenger is also used by many children and teenagers. These are all free to use but you must be aware of the possible dangers of some social networking sites. If you are concerned, there are many guidelines to help. www.kidshield.co.uk has some great advice and advocates the use of parental control software (for example, Net Nanny at £29.99).

Shockingly, there are many reports of paedophiles paying young people to perform in front of web cameras. Teens feel safe in their bedrooms and are often enticed by the lure of money or gifts. Some people have suggested placing the computer (if using a webcam) in a living area rather than the child or teenager's bedroom to help deter any possible paedophile. Tell your child never to reply to unknown emails and educate your child in the correct procedures to follow when online. Do not bury this under the carpet and hope that your child is too clever to fall for these scams. The abusers are always one step ahead. Education is the best prevention.

The following guidelines have been put together by www.Kidshield.co.uk

How can you protect your children who use Social Networking sites?
- Limit the amount of personal information posted. Educate your children to limit the amount of information they post that could make them vulnerable (e.g. full name, address, information about routines). If their friends or connections post information about them, make sure the combined information is not more than they would be comfortable with strangers knowing.
- Remember that the internet is a public resource. Educate your children to only post information they are comfortable with anyone seeing. This includes

information in their profile and in blogs and other forums.

- Be wary of strangers. The internet makes it easy for people to misrepresent their identities and motives. Educate your children to consider limiting the people who are allowed to contact them on these sites.
- Be aware. Educate your children to be aware of potential online predators. People may post false or misleading information about various topics, including their own identities.
- Check privacy policies. As a parent, educator or carer, be aware that some sites may share information such as email addresses or user preferences with other companies; your children should be alerted to this potential hazard. Try to locate the policy for handling referrals to make sure that your children do not unintentionally sign up their friends for spam emails. Some sites will continue to send email messages to anyone you refer until they join.

Children are especially susceptible to the threats that social networking sites present. Although many of these sites have age restrictions, children may misrepresent their ages so that they can join. By teaching children about internet safety, being aware of their online habits, and guiding them to appropriate sites, parents can make sure that their children become safe and responsible users.

Games consoles

Games consoles and games are on most children's wish list. Find the best deals for games consoles by using comparison websites. If you are buying online, don't forget to use a price checker such as Twenga (www.twenga.co.uk) or www.pricechecker.co.uk You may get an even better deal by then looking for a link to the best deal from a cash-back website (see Chapter 12 for more information) but do your homework before committing. A recent report by *Which?* found that some deals through cash-back sites are not necessarily the cheapest around.

Alternatively, some retailers sell used consoles (often with three-month warranties) for a reduced price. The best time to get a bargain on a trade in is after a new console has been launched.

Games can range from a few pounds up to £45. Wii, PS3 and Xbox are the leading platforms, but PC games have had a bit of a comeback – ensure you have the correct software on your computer before purchasing. I would recommend hiring a game. Libraries, Blockbusters and online DVD hire companies such as LoveFilm offer some great deals. Alternatively, buy from retailers such as Gamestation, who are happy to exchange if the game is not suitable. They also offer traded games for less, saving more money.

Just like clothing swap parties, you could encourage your children to trade their games, CDs and DVDs around their friends – though monitor this to ensure they are not being ripped off! When a game is no longer being played and they are gagging for the next best thing, encourage them to sell before purchasing the next one. EBay, Amazon and even the local paper are great. Game retailers may buy back a game and offer a better price if you're buying another game from them but, be aware, they add their own mark-up so their offer may be much lower than selling privately. Other alternatives are swap shops such as www.swapitshop.co.uk

TV, DVD and cinema

If your child desires their own TV in their bedroom, avoid adding them to your TV subscription. Sky charge £10 a month for multi-room use, yet for less than a £20 one off fee you can purchase a Freeview box. If they have their own computer, they can access many TV programmes online for free. BBC iPlayer allows you to catch up with all TV programmes in the last seven days; ITV Player and 4oD (Channel 4) for up to 30 days. Sky Player is available to everyone for free.

DVDs cost up to £20 each and may have limited viewing. Again, encourage your child to trade in and sell unwanted items. If they are keen to get the latest blockbuster, why not sign up for DVD rental. There are some fantastic deals to be had, including 30-day free trials. There is nothing stopping you from being a bit of a rental tart and trying all these free services before committing ... that will keep you busy for several months. Remember though to cancel each one before moving on or you could be in for some bills! www.uk-dvd-rental-guide.com and www.dvdgenie.co.uk are great comparison sites.

Libraries are great for DVD and CD rental. The rental

period is usually for a week for DVDs and longer for CDs. They are often much cheaper than high street rental companies, plus you can try to encourage your child or teen to grab some free books while they are there!

If they love the cinema, why not sign them up for some of the deals. Orange Wednesday offers free cinema tickets for two every Wednesday (and buy one get one free on pizzas).

Book worms

I am a complete book addict and I have encouraged my children to follow suit. From a very early age, we have visited the library and enjoyed sharing books. As a family, we probably read around ten books a month, maybe more. I buy a huge amount from charity shops or boot sales, often picking up bargains for as little as 10p.

I do buy new books as I am impatient to read the latest bestseller, but I always try to get the best deal. I have joined free book clubs, such as WHSmith Privilege club, to receive great discounts, but do search for prices before buying as online retailers are often cheaper. I always ensure the books are well cared for and I sell them when read. In some instances, I have even made a profit! Asda usually have the latest best selling paperbacks for less than £4 each, with Tesco coming a close second for price.

There are book swap sites and shops on the high street offering a read and return service.

Exercise some power

Obesity is a real problem in this country. We spend more time than ever before sitting on our backsides. I am as guilty as everyone is and I do suffer from writers' bottom and belly, caused by too much time sitting on my backside eating chocolate. Children and teenagers need to be encouraged to get out and exercise, but don't just point the finger at them – make this a family activity. You could cycle together (if you don't have bikes, look in your local paper for a used one, or put a request on Freecycle).

Swimming is fantastic exercise and your local swimming pool may have offers and discounts for students, families and regular users. www.swim4fitness.com offers free swimming sessions and advice, so it is well worth registering.

One of the best things to come out of a games console is the Nintendo Wii. If you have never used one before, be prepared to ache the next day (unless you are an uber cool teenager who manages to play all games with a mere flick of the wrist). I love Wii Fit and really should spend more time on it. The sports games are great for bonding as a family; beware of obstacles, breakages and accidents as you can get carried away. For very young children, VTech have launched a similar console.

Great days out

As Janey has already mentioned, museums are free and offer great days out for kids. Don't stop going as your child gets older. Find out what interests them, or even what projects they are working on at school, and incorporate this into a great day out.

If you and your children have a favourite TV show, why not see if you can be a member of the audience. Many shows offer free audience tickets. For more information, visit the TV website. Other sites of interest include www.applausestore.com, www.sroaudiences.com and www.tvrecordings.com

If you have access to the internet, visit www.dofreestuff.com – a great website for a quick and easy search and you will find lots of free things to do in your area. A new site offering discounts on days out across the UK is www.contigreatdaysout.co.uk

Get back to nature and enjoy the peace and tranquillity of the great outdoors! We live in a beautiful country and often don't appreciate what is around us. Gorgeous beaches, moors, forests and the most amazing walks – and all for free. Pack a flask and some sandwiches and enjoy some family time.

Voluntary work is so rewarding and can be hugely enjoyable, so why not encourage your teenager to get involved. If they have plans to attend university, this will be a valuable addition to their CV. Visit www.do-it.org for more information.

Cheap holidays and activities

I have included this here rather than in Chapter 10 as it is more relevant. There are some great holidays just for kids, a bit like summer camps. www.campbeaumont.co.uk offer some great activity holidays from as little as £59 per child for a week. www.summerfunkids.co.uk is a great directory of kids' activities and summer camps. I like the National Trust Working holidays (www.nationaltrust.org), which now allow family holidays. These holidays are for parents and up to three children aged between 8 and 16 years. Tasks may include vegetation clearance, creating deadwood habitat piles and beach clearance. There will also be a chance to explore the area where you are staying either on foot or on bike. Accommodation is comfortable style hostel accommodation, shared with three other families.

There are also many organisations offering kids' activities during the school holidays, and some are free. Speak to your school and local council for information on what is happening in your area.

Teenage Angst

Any parent who has lived through the teenage years knows what a challenge it can be. Teenagers are getting younger all the time, with moody sulks and demands starting as young as ten years old. It can be an expensive time for any parent, as demands rise along with your bundle of rebellion's need to be what they want to be – which inevitably involves money!

The bedroom trap

It is a common complaint that I hear from every parent of a teenager: 'We never see them; they spend all their time in their bedrooms glued to a screen'. I don't think we can ignore the pull of the computer or game consoles for our teens and, if we were honest with ourselves, would we prefer them to be on the street or sitting with us moaning? Having said that, I do think we need to entice them out of their holes when we can. I refuse to let my children eat their meals anywhere other than the dining room table.

Family mealtimes are so important. It encourages conversation and a feeling of being a family unit. Talk to them and find out what their interests are. Encourage and discover these interests with them, and do not be afraid to praise them when necessary. Despite the sulks and grunts, you may find they actually would like your friendship.

Teach your children well

If you are lucky enough to have raised your children with great values and acceptance for the outdoor life, the teenage years may be a breeze. But before you sit back, relax and gloat, beware that one night your little darling will go to bed and the next day you will wake up to find a stranger has taken over their body. It happened to me. Suddenly my angelic son became a long-haired, smelly, moody teen with a love of Nirvana. The saving grace is his hatred of all things designer, so thankfully our shopping days are spent in charity shops and vintage sales.

If you have daughters, why not teach them how to make their own cosmetics. My friends' daughters love combining a sleep over with a DIY pampering session. Teach them how to adapt their own clothing to create individual fashion pieces and encourage them to get more for their money with vintage, charity and boot sale bargains.

Hard-life lessons

One of the most useful lessons for a teenager to learn is the ability to earn their own money and stand on their own two feet. It does not matter if this is a Saturday job, a paper round or earning pocket money for jobs around the house. When I was growing up I wanted everything and I wanted it now! My mum decided to give me my share of the child benefit but, in return, I had to buy all my clothes and everything else I wanted or needed – I could not ask for anything. It was a good lesson and, coupled with my weekend jobs, I soon learnt the value of money and how to take control of my finances. As Janey says earlier in this chapter, get your children used to donating or even selling their old toys and, by the time they become teenagers, they can apply this principle to their console games, books and music to earn extra cash.

Money matters for teens

Once you have taught them the value of money, they might need to be let loose in the big wide world with their own cash. I love prepaid credit and debit cards. Simply top them up and they are ready for use. They are a great way to avoid teens carrying around cash, especially when they are on holiday or days out. Check out www.what-prepaid-card.co.uk for more information and the latest deals.

Music downloads

Music plays an important role in the teen's life. CDs are becoming a thing of the past, with music downloads becoming the personal choice. ITunes is still one of the favourite choices but it can be expensive to download full albums. Singles cost around 79p a track but it still adds up. With internet providers clamping down on illegal downloads, you really have to be aware of where the music is coming from. It is illegal to share music and download illegally. The rule is that unless the artist is receiving payment, you are downloading illegally. This applies to file-sharing sites – even those to which you pay to subscribe, such as LimeWire.

MusicStation, which is available on Vodafone UK mobiles, lets you download unlimited amounts of music from an extensive catalogue of over 3 million tracks, over the air without the need to connect to a PC and broadband. You can also view the latest charts, share playlists with other users, read all the gossip on favourite artists as well as find about out gig dates. All this will cost you just £1.95 per week and there are no hidden data charges. It is available on over 40 different Vodafone mobiles and is apparently more popular than Napster in the UK. At less than £10 a month, you can have unlimited legal downloads, which is less than the price of one album. Spotify is great for listening to the latest music free via your PC.

Datz Music Lounge costs £99.99 for the software and 'security dongle' necessary to access the music service for a whole year and legally download as many tracks as you like. Since most legal downloads cost in the region of 70p per track, you can rapidly recoup your initial investment.

Driving us mad

As 17 approaches, every parent starts to dread the driving lessons. I thought I was pretty cool about the whole thing until I got into the car with my son and realised I had no brake! Then came the reality of the expense. Driving lessons are vital but can be very costly. One cheaper alternative is to pay for an intensive course of lessons, which includes the test at the end. Hopefully, they will then pass. The key is not to wait until this time, but to budget. I have a savings account for my youngest already started for when his turn comes.

We decided to buy a cheap and economic car for our son to run around in. The insurance was made more reasonable by adding our names to the policy. However, the day he passed his test we were in for a shock. The premium tripled! We brought this down by searching for new insurers and putting him through the Pass Plus training course, but it is still double what I pay for my car. Had we not lived in a remote area, I would not have purchased a car for him. It is too expensive and insurance companies are reluctant to give any discounts until the drivers are at least 21 years old.

CHAPTER NINE

Transport

'TRAVEL TEACHES TOLERATION.'
Benjamin Disraeli

We all need transport. Whether it is car, rail, aeroplane or bus, it is a vital part of our everyday lives. However, the expense can often be crippling. Is there another way? Not really, but with a little savvy thinking you can at least help to reduce the expense.

Cars

Cars can be a money pit, but they are a part of our lives. Look at how you use your car. Do you have more than one car in your household? Is the second car used regularly? Are there ways you can cut your expenditure? Could you use public transport or share your car? Here are some tips to help keep your car costs low.

Buying a new car

If you're buying a new car, make sure you do your homework before you buy. Look at reviews such as Parker's (www.parkers.co.uk) or www.whatcar.com which both show you the true costs of the car plus full review. They also show the rate of depreciation, which is so important if you are looking at trading in the vehicle within the next three years. Talk to the dealer to find out the cost of the tax, insurance group and the best MPG (miles per gallon).

Car dealers are having a hard time in the recession. Take advantage of this by asking for the best price and extras. They may throw in a year's car tax, a full tank of petrol or add an option to your car. You can also phone What Car? Target Price on 0845 272 6000 and they will tell you the dealer's discount and how low they will really go on price. Search online to find the best deal. If you find it cheaper elsewhere, go back to you local dealer and renegotiate.

If you are trading in your old car, be prepared with the correct trade-in valuation. Again, Parker's or What Car? can help with this. Dealers will try to knock you down but stand firm. If you know your car is worth a certain price, make sure you are happy with the price you are offered. Sometimes it is better to sell privately as you will get more for your car. Remember presentation is everything. Clean your car or have it valeted to ensure the best price. Stale cigarette and dog smells are a real turn-off for some buyers, so clean and freshen it well.

Buying a used car

Just because you're buying a used car, it does not mean you can't adopt the same principles described above. Always negotiate and always do your homework. If you are looking for a specific car, check the prices by using car guides such as Parker's or Glass's (www.glass.co.uk) to make sure you are paying the correct price for your car's condition. You can also download a buying guide for your specific type of car – pointing out what to look for when viewing ... essential reading! EBay and Auto Trader (www.autotrader.co.uk) are also great places to search for a car, even if you do not intend to buy from them. They will show you price and availability and, by reading the write-ups, you can find out about any areas of concern.

If you are buying from a private or an unauthorised dealer, always do a HPI check which can reveal the history of the car, particularly if it has been stolen, written off or has outstanding finance. You can do a HPI check for as little as £3.95 – well worth the money to ensure your car is all it is reputed to be. If you are spending a lot of money, it may be worth getting an AA or RAC inspection. Prices start from £130. If the seller is not keen to allow this, they obviously have something to hide so walk away.

Check all the documents match the car's mileage and vehicle identification number. Don't accept any excuse for missing documents – simply walk away. Take the car for a test drive and try the gears, brakes, oil, water, belts, electrics and any other gadget that comes with the car. Ask for the car history and read this carefully. Motors.co.uk offer some great advice (www.motors.co.uk/cars/buying-advice).

Classic cars

If you buy a classic or heritage car, you can make massive savings. If the car is registered before 1973, it is exempt from tax. Insurance for classic vehicles is also dramatically cheaper. I have owned many classic cars – all modest but gorgeous cars such as Austin A35s, a Mini and a Morris Minor. Insurance cost me less than £100 for a year, fully comprehensive with breakdown cover! Maintenance is straightforward on these older cars – no expensive computers or electronics to go wrong. Plus, they will always raise a smile from onlookers. I could never drive anywhere without someone stopping me to reminisce.

Insurance

You must have got the message by now: use online search engines to find ways to reduce your insurance premium – they really do work and are very simple to use. Sites such as www.gocompare.com and www.moneysupermarket.com will save you money. The other advantage is that, once registered, you don't have to go through the same endless questions again and again, as the site stores your information.

Don't get stuck in a rut with your existing company. Just because they were the cheapest one year, this does not make them the cheapest all the time. My insurance policy has just been due for renewal. I checked last year to find the cheapest, and when I checked again this year I found I could save almost £200 more with a different company. For the sake of ten minutes of my time, I have saved over £20 a month. If you don't have access to the internet – go to the library and ask them to help you. It really is worth the visit. If you want to opt for an eco company, go to www.ibuyeco.co.uk which claims to offer 100% carbon neutral car insurance.

Direct Line Insurance has kindly given me the following tips to help reduce your insurance.

- Ensure that only people who drive regularly are named on the policy. You can always add someone for a few days when they really need to drive the car.
- Protect your No Claim Discount. It may increase the premium by a few pounds, but this fades into insignificance against the potential loss of a 65% discount on a premium of several hundred pounds.
- Agree to accept an excess on your policy. This means that you will agree to pay a specified amount towards the cost of a claim. If you are not at fault

in an accident the excess can be recovered.

- Agree to a mileage restriction. The fewer the miles the car covers, the greater the saving.
- If you decide to change your car, check with your insurer if the model will have a significant effect on the premium. Sporty cars can attract a high premium and often a slightly different model or smaller engine can make a big difference.
- If you have a garage, clear out all of your junk and use it for your car. Aside from the benefit of not having to scrape the ice off in the winter, there is a higher risk of theft by keeping the car on the road, so keeping it in the garage will be reflected in your premium.

Fuel and running costs

Prevention is better than cure and, in terms of your car, prevention is definitely cheaper than solving a problem. The RAC has helped me put together some useful tips to help reduce your fuel and running costs.

- Keep the pressure up. Dropping just 10 psi under the vehicle manufacturer's recommended tyre pressure can increase fuel consumption by 2.5%.
- You may think there is not much you can do to save on fuel, but you are wrong. The fantastic website www.petrolprices.com allows you to check the best prices in your area – it is simple and free to use.
- Reduce your speed. For example, driving at 70 mph

rather than 85 mph is up to 25% more efficient and happens to be legal!

- Don't drive too close to the vehicle in front; you'll end up constantly breaking and then having to accelerate. Smooth driving at a constant speed is the most fuel-efficient way to drive.
- Likewise, anticipate traffic. A constantly moving car is better than one that keeps starting and stopping.
- Keep the revs down. Look to change up gear at lower revs (approximately 2k revs for diesel, 2.5k for petrol).
- Don't let your engine idle for too long. Switch it off when it's safe to do so.
- Go easy on the air conditioning. It's a drain on your system and can boost fuel consumption by up to 10%.
- Reverse park your car. Reversing out of a space when your engine is cold uses up to 25 times more petrol than when it's warm.
- Only switch your engine on when you are ready to go and don't leave it to warm up – it's a big waste of fuel. Just drive off gently for the first few minutes so the engine gradually warms up.
- Cold engines use more fuel so avoid unnecessary revving on cold mornings to try and speed up the car's heater and demisting function.
- Don't avoid a service. Regular servicing is the important factor to highlight and, while this doesn't necessarily make the vehicle more efficient, it helps prevent it from becoming inefficient (for example, by checking fouled spark plugs, air filters, etc). It

will also mean your car is safer and retains its value better, as well as avoiding little problems being left unchecked and turning into bigger ones that are more expensive to solve!

- Ring round for the best price on spare parts. However, be careful not to invalidate your car warranty if you have one.
- Check your oil, coolant and brake fluids regularly to avoid problems and big bills!
- Wash your car yourself. Not only will you save the cost of a car or jet wash, but you'll also improve the aerodynamics and help avoid the potential build up of nasty chemicals that can cause erosion of your paint work!
- Keep the weight down. Don't carry unnecessary weight around and don't fully fill up your petrol tank either – it all means your engine has to work harder.
- Get rid of the roof rack when it is not in use. It affects the aerodynamics of your vehicle, as do open windows and sunroofs.
- Keep all bills, services and documents for your car. When you come to sell, this will be a big plus for a buyer and could add value to your car.

Tax doesn't have to be taxing

You know you have to tax your car so avoid the mad last minute rush to find the money. Budget! Open a savings account or a prepaid credit card and put the money away every month. Alternatively buy £5 savings stamps from your post office. You can save by buying annually and online. If you are buying a new car, take advantage of the low carbon tax bonuses. Many cars are now nil tax or only £35 a year. Pre 2001 cars are at a fixed rate for under 1549cc and over 1549cc. Cars under 1549cc are cheaper to tax than larger engine sizes. Those registered after 2001 are taxed according to the CO_2 emissions.

Don't breakdown

Breakdown cover is a great asset but, as with everything, do your homework and make sure you are getting the best deal. You can buy breakdown cover direct from organisations such as AA or RAC, or you can add to your insurance premium. Read the small print before signing up to any deal. I noticed that my breakdown cover limited me to a number of breakdowns per year before I was charged, yet through my insurance the cover was unlimited. You can get breakdown cover for your car or for you personally – meaning any car you are travelling in is covered. www.breakdownrecovery.co.uk or the usual comparison websites will compare and find the best option for you.

Share the load

If you commute to work, why not share the costs and join a car share scheme? Contact your local council for details. Alternatively go to www.nationalcarshare.co.uk or www.isanyonegoingto.com for more information and advice.

Car rental

If you live in a city and only use a car occasionally, it is probably worth your while hiring a car on an as and when needed basis. Do your sums to ensure this is the best route for you. There is no point paying tax, insurance, MOT, car parking and maintenance costs if you only use the car once a month. www.carplus.org calculates that, if you drive less than 6,000 miles per year, a car club could save you up to £3,500 a year. Replacing a second family car with car club membership is likely to bring even more cash savings.

www.citycarclub.co.uk is a great company that offers no hassle car rental to its members. Hertz have recently launched a car-sharing club called Connect by Hertz, which saves members money on car ownership.

Rail

Apparently, we have the highest costing rail service in Europe. I know this very well having had to travel from Devon to London on a regular basis. Aiming to get to London before 11.30am, I would have to part with over £200 for a return ticket. It is crazy to think that I could have travelled halfway across the world for the same price. There are ways to cut the cost of the ticket. Here are some tips.

- Buy in advance whenever possible. Even buying the day before can give you great savings.
- Look at the price of two single tickets. Sometimes this is far cheaper than the cost of a return, especially if one part of your journey incorporates peak time travel.
- Sadly, regular travellers do not get any discount cards but you may be able to buy season tickets or local rail

cards. Speak to your nearest station or go to www.nationalrail.co.uk If you travel with a child, are disabled, a student or old age pensioner, you will be eligible for a railcard. This can give you over a third off rail costs. Use it to book tickets in advance and your savings will be even greater. Virgin Trains allow railcard holders to travel in peak periods with walk-up off-peak tickets.

- Avoid travelling at peak times unless you can really help it. Sometimes you can travel on an alternative route to avoid the peak time charges when entering a city.
- Sometimes, bizarrely, splitting your journey and buying separate tickets for each part can work out a lot cheaper than one return ticket. There are many rail websites (such as www.thetrainline.com and www.nationalrail.co.uk) with which you can compare the return price with single split prices. The key is to do your homework before you book.
- To avoid calling the 0845 748 4950 number for national rail enquiries, keep the direct number handy on your mobile: 0121 634 2040 followed by 1, when prompted, will take you through to the number you require. (Thanks to www.saynoto0870.com for this tip.)

Flying

Air travel has become quite competitive with companies like easyJet and Ryanair making air travel more affordable to the masses. If you are a frequent traveller, sign up to the newsletters from your local airline. Ryanair constantly have sales with massively reduced seats. I have bought seats for as little as 1p including taxes, and paying with a Visa Electron card incurs no extra charge. As with rail travel, the key is to book as far in advance as possible.

If you know where you want to go, you can use flight checkers or airlines' own search engines. Again, www.moneysavingexpert.com has a wonderful flight checker tool that can save you money. As with everything, shop around to get the best deal for you. Also try www.travelsupermarket.com and www.cheapflights.co.uk

CHAPTER TEN

Holidays

'My heart is warm with the friends
I make, And better friends I'll not
be knowing; Yet there isn't a train
I wouldn't take, No matter
where it's going.'
Edna St Vincent Millay

We all want to kick back, relax and enjoy a lovely holiday but do our finances allow it? I have been caught in the trap where I have not budgeted and suddenly summer is upon us and I can then no longer afford to pay for a holiday. The key is to budget and plan in advance. Some people book their holiday almost a year in advance, giving them more months to pay for the annual holiday without the last minute stress.

There are some great forums and advice websites for help when choosing a holiday, particularly if you have a small family. www.takethefamily.com is a fantastic website for family holiday ideas, great places to go (UK and abroad), holiday advice and forums for families to share their holiday experiences.

There are other ways to enjoy a holiday, even on a budget.

Holiday Swaps

It may sound a bit worrying but holiday swaps are a great and affordable way to enjoy a holiday. There are many companies offering this service. You simply list your property as honestly as possible and find a suitable family to swap with. All you pay for is your travelling expenses.

Jackie and Dave Wiltshire from Harlech, Gwynedd in North Wales went on three swaps through friends-of-friends before turning the house swap concept into a dedicated website: www.UKHolidaySwapShop.co.uk They offer the following advice.

'When we first swapped we found it took a bit of effort to get the house in order. If you go on an ordinary holiday you would just go, but with swapping you have to make sure everything is nice, put any valuables away, and that anything that needs fixing has been fixed,' says Jackie.

'But once the house is done it's done and, the people you swap with do the same, so when you get to their house it's very homely. Often self-catering places are so clinical – there's nothing in them. It's nice to stay somewhere homely.

'We went to South Wales and Dorset, and we also stayed near Leamington Spa where Dave went to university. We didn't stay in the houses much, we just used them for a base but the experience was great. We did chip a plate once and felt terrible, which caused a bit of stress. But we bought them a new crockery set so they didn't mind.'

Most people would worry about having strangers in their home but, from the holiday swappers I have spoken to, by the time you are making the swap, you have become good friends. Also, remember that while they are in your home, you are in theirs, so the risk is equal. Jackie offers the following advice on this concern.

'We urge all our swappers to notify their house insurance company about their swap. Most house insurances cover "invited guests" – but it is best to check with them first. We suggest people put away items of sentimental or intrinsic value in preparation of a swap, for example in a locked room. There is a comprehensive "guide to happy swapping" and FAQs on the website, offering information for people wishing to swap their home for the purpose of a holiday.'

Other sites include:
- www.homexchangevacation.com
- www.homebase-hols.com
- www.1sthomeexchange.com

Working Holidays

Working holidays have been around for many years. Kent was a great location for Londoners to escape the smog and have some fun in the garden of England. Hop picking was very popular. More common now is grape picking in France or you could even go as far afield as Australia (see www.working-holidays.co.uk). You could become a chambermaid and get free skiing in exchange for cleaning toilets and waiting on guests.

The National Trust (www.nationaltrust.org.uk) runs around 400 working holidays every year throughout England, Wales and Northern Ireland. Whether you fancy carrying out a survey of moorland plants or herding goats, dry stonewalling or organic gardening, there will be something to suit you and all in stunning countryside or coastal locations. Some holidays allow you to combine activities such as surfing, horse riding and digital photography with conservation tasks for a varied week. They also offer family holidays, which are perfect to get your children involved in conservation issues.

Hobby Holidays

There are many great holidays where you can indulge in your favourite hobby. This could be a cookery course, painting, wine tasting or even a writer's workshop. Whatever you choose, you will be sure of meeting like-minded friends. www.theholidaydirectory.co.uk is a great site to find the activity or hobby holiday of your choice.

Hostels

Hostels are not just for the youth. You can visit a hostel at any age and even with children – though I would insist on a private family room if you have children, rather than sharing a dorm with strangers. Prices are very cheap and accommodation is much improved, with cooking facilities, private rooms and even sometimes ensuites. They are a great idea if you are touring or just staying one or two nights. Visit www.yha.org.uk, www.hostelclub.com and www.hostelworld.com for more information and great deals.

Camping and Caravanning

According to statistics, the number of enquiries for campervans, motor homes and caravans has dramatically increased since the recession has hit. Visit Britain found 1 in 5 Brits who holidayed overseas in 2008 are now thinking of spending their summer holidays in the UK. I love camping and have spent fantastic holidays with my family in our vintage caravan. There is something magical about the smell of a cooked breakfast prepared on the gas hob when camping. We used to be members of the Caravan Club – certainly not all Harold and Hilda types. It enabled us to visit more obscure and remote club sites, often with less than five pitches on the site. For around £5 a night, it is an absolute bargain.

You don't have to be an ardent camper or caravan enthusiast to enjoy camping. There are now luxury campsites across Europe catering to your every need. I love Canvas Holidays. They now offer the most amazing fairy tale packages – tree houses, Hansel and Gretel cottages, luxury cabins and even gypsy caravans. Visit www.canvasholidays.co.uk for more information. Other great companies include Keycamp (www.keycamp.co.uk) and Eurocamp (www.eurocamp.co.uk).

If you like the idea of a holiday on the road but cannot afford your own mobile home, why not rent one? You can hire 1960s VW campers right through to the celebrity status Winnebago and Airstream caravans.

Budget Holiday Deals

The key to getting great deals is to book very early or, if you don't really care where you go, you can get some last minute bargains. Package holidays include flight, accommodation and transfers and usually last 7 or 14 days. You may think they have fixed prices but you will be surprised. I remember seeing a TV programme where they asked holidaymakers in one hotel to divulge the price they paid. The results were quite shocking, ranging from under £200 right up to almost £800 – all for the same holiday. Obviously, destination and timing plays a huge part in the deals – school holidays will always be a premium for popular family destinations.

The main tour operators have some fantastic deals, or visit your local travel agent for information. Do your homework first and don't be afraid to haggle and play one deal off with another.

If you have a family, you may prefer self-catering and even the luxury of your own villa with a pool. These are surprisingly cheap if you book direct with the owners. At the time of writing, you can get deals for a week's accommodation from as little as £250. You have to book your own flights and transfers but, with a little organisation, this is a great option. There are tour operators who specialise in villa holidays if you want to get a package deal.

Weekend breaks

There are excellent deals to be had for weekend breaks. As with holidays, last minute bargains are always available. www.lastminute.com, www.hotel.com and www.expedia.com are good sites for finding the deals. www.moneysavingexpert.com highlights the best hotel deals, so it is worth subscribing to the weekly email to be notified.

Do your homework

You can buy from your travel agent, but often the best deals are available direct from the holiday company or as last minute offers. www.ebookers.com, www.lastminute.com, www.expedia.com, www.travel.co.uk, www.co-operative-travel.co.uk, www.holidayholiday.co.uk, www.traveleconomy.com and www.travelsupermarket.com are great sites to help you search for the perfect holiday and save money.

Teletext is still a popular and useful resource for finding bargains. If you prefer to book direct with your local travel agency, use Teletext first to give you an idea of prices.

It is also worth looking at the national newspapers. *The Sun* promotes some very cheap holiday deals. Simply collect the vouchers and book the holiday. *The Telegraph* is also a great paper in which to look for deals (go online to www.telegraph.co.uk).

Eco Holidays

Green holidays are becoming more and more popular. This does not mean staying in a yurt eating lentils – you can have the highest luxury and still help the planet. I really like www.ecoholidaying.co.uk It offers some fantastic advice and reference for anyone wishing to embark on an eco break. Another great site for inspiration is www.imaginative-traveller.com Closer to home you can opt to stay on organic farms, in eco cottages and even in horse-drawn caravans. www.ecoescapes.org is a wonderful site and the accompanying travel guides (£8.99) contain some very useful information for eco travelling in the UK.

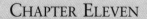

CHAPTER ELEVEN

Make Do and Mend

'NO MATTER HOW OLD YOU GET, IF YOU
CAN KEEP THE DESIRE TO BE CREATIVE,
YOU'RE KEEPING THE MAN-CHILD ALIVE.'
John Cassavetes

We have become a throw away culture. Do we know how to maintain or repair things anymore? Schools no longer teach practical skills to our children. We have lost the ability to mend things. This could be cars, electrical or even how to fix a leaking tap. We are too hasty to call out a repairman or simply throw the items away. I have been guilty of throwing perfectly good clothes away simply because a zip or buttons had fallen off. I would convince myself it was past its best and look forward to buying the replacement. It is only when you start to look at how we lead our lives, we truly realise the money we are wasting.

Repair, Reduce, Reuse, Recycle

Recently my dishwasher died after only 14 months since buying it new. The local repairman wanted a £120 call-out fee without including the price for any new parts. With new models starting at £150, it makes it difficult to warrant a repair. It makes me so mad. Companies should either ensure that their products function for longer than a year, or help customers repair them at reasonable cost. With mounting frustration, I searched the internet and found a forum talking about problems with the particular make and model I had and how to solve them. With no experience, we decided to try to repair the machine. I located the necessary part (at a cost of £20) and my husband, who is a self-confessed bodger, attempted to fit it. With fingers and toes crossed, we finally succeeded. For £20, a few swear words and an hour's work, we saved over £130.

There has been a revival in crafts, knitting and sewing. We are looking more at making our own unique items, particularly with fashion. If you cannot afford the latest designer trend, adapt a piece of clothing to make your unique style and statement. I love the book *House Proud: Hip Craft for the Modern Homemaker* by Danielle Proud as it is packed full of great ideas with realistic projects even for the beginner. *Yeah, I Made it Myself: DIY Fashion for the Not Very Domestic Goddess* by Eithne Farry is another great book for those who want to dip their toes into the world of sewing and crafts. A fantastic website for ideas, tips and inspiration is www.designspongeonline.com but, beware, it is seriously addictive!

My parents and I recently converted the old family slides into a digital format. Photos that had been lost for the last 25 years were suddenly brought to life. One of the things we noticed was our clothing, particularly mine as I was growing up. Dresses in one photo became tops in another. Trousers became shorts. There was even clothing made from curtains, which made my mum laugh. When I was a teenager, I would want the latest style, but often we were unable to afford it. We would visit the local haberdashery store, buy a pattern and fabric, and make the skirt or top copying the designer trends. I had the latest fashion but in my own unique style – my friends were envious.

Michelle Redmond is a keen money saver and environmentalist. Running a busy PR company and caring for her small children leaves her little time for sewing projects, but she has found a solution.

'Find a good dressmaker. I just found a gem of a lady by chance living round the corner. She is a pattern maker and tailor who does costumes for big film sets etc and she is a whizz at altering garments. I've just had a jacket tailored to me – the skirt fitted and the jacket didn't so had been sitting in the closet for ages ruining what should have been a fab suit. It cost me £8. She is about to take in two large pairs of trousers that I had to wear post babies. They are a lovely cut but don't look good now I'm trimmer, so she's going to take them down a dress size.

'All those old suits with padded shoulders – she can take the pads out and re-tailor them. She can also fit shirts that weren't previously fitted. If you have fabric that you like in an outdated trend, she can make it into something else! I found her on Netmums!

'So, my tip for an instant makeover is to find a good dressmaker to revamp your wardrobe of nice but outdated or ill-fitting clothes rather than buying cheap new clothes!'

I have been reading through some old war books. Prepared by the Ministry of Information for the Board of Trade in 1943, *Make Do and Mend* is a fantastic book and I believe you can buy copies from Amazon for £4.99. It contains tips on how to look after your clothes, washing and ironing and ways of turning old items into something new. It goes to prove the point that we have become complacent in our throw away culture and really a bit lazy. The time we spend watching mindless TV, we could be spending on our homes, lifestyle and even turning our hobbies or crafts into extra cash.

While trawling through the internet, I found the website for Lewes District Council. They have a page called 'Make Do and Mend' (www.lewes.gov.uk/environment/9559.asp) and it has some fantastic tips. They estimate that we could reduce our rubbish generation by 15% by following the reuse, repair and recycle route. Their site even includes local trades people for repairs – I am seriously impressed and would urge all councils to follow suit.

Join the network

There are some great networks across the country offering support, friendship and ideas. Stitch and Bitch groups are a modern take on the historical embroidery and sewing women's groups from bygone eras. Speak to your nearest haberdashery or wool shop for more information on what is happening in your area.

Learn a new skill

Whether your interest is a craft, dressmaking, plumbing or motor mechanics, there is probably a course at your local college. Not only will you gain a new skill, save money on repairs and projects, you could also offer your services to others to earn extra money. The cost of the course will soon be repaid with dividends.

Alternatively explore your local craft shop. You will find home kits for most simple crafts. Candle making, knitting, jewellery making, crochet, woodwork, glass painting – the list is endless. If, like me, you love scented candles, why not make your own? You can buy the wicks and wax from your local craft store, add some essential oils, and pour into readymade moulds, even old china cups or pretty flameproof containers.

Share your skills

There are many great schemes available for those who want to share their skills. The LETS (Local Exchange Trading) schemes trade in their own currency – simply trade skills or services in your area. Some communities also have bartering systems. www.oddjobswap.co.uk is a website created to help you swap your talents and abilities with other people locally. BT offers a great service (http://bttradespace.com). They say that 'BTTradespace is an online community that brings businesses and their customers together to do business and build lasting, relevant relationships.'

Make Your Own Gifts

Finding the perfect gift can be quite a challenge. Our high streets are all full of the same shops selling the same old rubbish. Nothing is unique anymore. I personally hate the buy three for two deals promoted by some of the larger stores. You know when you receive them that they were mindless purchases, with the sole aim of trying to save money rather than thinking of the receiver. It is much nicer to give a gift you have spent time with, even if it costs very little. It really is the thought that counts.

If you are going to give a homemade gift, spend time on the wrapping. A gorgeously wrapped gift means so much, and will always delight and impress the receiver. I buy florist cellophane and decorative ribbons from eBay. Brown paper can also look great, particularly when used with coloured twine, twisted with some green foliage. Here are a few suggestions for some wonderful gifts.

• Homemade gifts really mean a lot. It could be a jar of jam or chutney, a cake, or even some delicious chocolates.

• Use some of the recipes in this book to make your own skincare products. Place in decorative pots and offer as gifts, though beware of use-by dates!

• Grow your own gifts. Bulbs planted in decorative pots, herbs grown in china teacups or a bunch of flowers from your garden are fantastic gifts. If you grow your own veg, why not put together a hamper of produce.

• Create your own experience day gift. Try a ramble, a picnic, a mystery tour or even a romantic stroll along the beach.

• Personalised gifts are very special, especially for family and loved ones. You can try your hand at creating your own DVD slide show of family photos (Nero is great software for this) or, if you aren't competent on the computer, you can use one of the many available companies to help. You can create calendars, photo books, mugs, t-shirts … the list is endless.

• Use your skills. You may be good at woodwork and could make a birdhouse or spice rack. Sewing experts can make beautiful lavender hearts or a beautiful shopping bag. Maybe you are passionate about genealogy. Why not trace friends' or families' family trees?

• Customise to create great gifts. You can buy cheap

plain t-shirts for children and appliqué some vintage or kids' fabric or motif on the front. You could buy a plain photo frame and personalise it, finishing it off by filling it with an appropriate photo.

- Use your computer. There are some fantastic packages and projects you can use via your computer and printer. Buy transfer paper to transform a plain item into a personal gift – cushion covers, bags and T-shirts can all look amazing with the right transfer.

- Hampers are great, but they don't have to be big to create a lovely gift. Collect baskets, gift boxes and ornate bags at boot sales and charity shops. Fill them with food, beauty products or even travel goodies for a personal gift. If the recipient has a hobby, why not collect some goodies to suit – gardeners, for example, would love seeds, gloves, soap and other fabulous gardening products. Package in beautiful cellophane and ribbons for a professional finish.

- An IOU gift may seem a bit cheeky but done right they can be great. Why not promise your loved one tea in bed for a week, or a 'Queen or King for the Day' treat when they don't not have to lift a finger.

Keep a drawer or box free to use as your gift collection. Fill this with items ready for Christmas and birthday gifts. Also keep a store of birthday cards, ribbons and wrapping. Collect items throughout the year so you always have a stash of gifts. If you are keeping gifts you received, make sure you note who gave them to you to avoid giving the item back to the same person!

CHAPTER TWELVE

Earning Extra Money

'LACK OF MONEY IS NO OBSTACLE.
LACK OF AN IDEA IS AN OBSTACLE.'
Ken Hakuta

Times are getting more difficult and we are now looking at finding extra incomes to survive. It is not unheard of for families to have two or three income streams coming in to their homes. Yorkshire Bank's quarterly Housebuyers' Report has revealed that 38% of people in the UK are turning to alternative ways to make money, from selling unwanted goods online to taking in lodgers. The most enterprising of UK regions is the South West, with 53% of those surveyed claiming they are trying to raise extra funds. The research has also revealed that the number of people trying to find new ways to raise extra money has increased by 26% between 2008 and 2009.

When I was growing up, my dad worked 12-hour days, Monday to Friday. At weekends, he would take extra work if needed in order to get us through some tough times. My mum would take in home-based work. We used to make the powder puffs that went into the fancy talc boxes and dress those hideous traditionally dressed dolls. This need to secure extra income has stayed with me. At 11 years old, I started my paper round. By the time I was 16, I had worked in a coffee shop, a garage serving petrol and an outlet making sausages. I also had a lucrative babysitting round in the village. By the time I reached 17 and studying my A levels, I had saved enough to buy my own car.

The most important advice I have been given was to always have more than one source of income as you never know when it will dry up. As a writer, I have to seek new opportunities in order to make a moderate living. I have been in the rat race – owning my own PR company and national magazine and the stress that went along with it all. I have chosen happiness over wealth and it works well for my family and me.

The key is to live the life you want to lead, be open-minded and flexible and don't spend your life struggling to live a lifestyle you can't afford. Step back and really look at your life. Are the hours and stress worth it all? Money is funny – the more you have, the more you spend. You still buy the same things; you just buy versions that are more expensive. Think about it. If you won the lottery tomorrow, what would you buy? A new car? A new house? A new watch? Suddenly Ferraris, million-pound mansions and Rolex watches are on your list. I am not knocking that, it is human nature, but until you win the lottery, keep your lifestyle within your budget.

Here are some avenues you could explore to help you earn some valuable extra income.

I Could Do That...

Have you ever said to yourself, 'I could do that' or that old favourite, 'That's money for old rope'? Do you sit in your office and dream of starting your own business? Every one of us has a talent; we just need to harness it. Maybe you love organising things, gardening, sewing, entertaining kids, working on computers or even interior design. Whatever it is you are passionate about, there may be a way to make this into a money-spinner. It does not have to be full-time; you could start by doing it in your spare time and build up a reputation for yourself.

I know friends who have started businesses from home.

They may not make huge amounts of money, particularly in the first few years, but they are much happier. People all over the country are turning their hobbies into businesses. One girl charged £35 an hour instructing others on how to use eBay in her spare time; a fashion student advertises herself as a personal shopper, helping women choose clothes that suit them. Why not become a wedding planner? The Wedding Planner School (www.theweddingplannerschool.org.uk) offers intensive weekend courses teaching people how to become wedding planners and set up their own businesses within the industry. A friend of mine makes wedding cakes and in the summer months she can easily turn around £1,000 a month just working in her spare time.

For more information and support have a look at www.moretolifethanshoes.com, www.mumsclub.co.uk, www.businesslink.gov.uk and www.hmrc.gov.uk

Think about the following questions before you begin.

- Identify your talent – is there a demand for this service?
- Identify your local competition – are they a threat or do you offer something unique?
- What are your start-up costs and when will you start making money?
- How much time and effort are you going to dedicate to this?
- What are your charges and are they correct for your service? If they are too low, you risk working for nothing; too high, and you will alienate new customers.

Keep Start-up Costs Low

Don't try to run before you can walk. The secret to a good business, even a part-time one, is to keep your overheads low and the cash flow high. You don't need to spend money on fancy all-singing all-dancing websites, laminated business cards or your own office. Think savvy...

Websites

You can get your own domain name and website building package online for as little as £19.99 from Mr Site (www.mrsite.co.uk) and also from computer stores. This payment will give you a year's service. Choose your domain name (www.yourname.co.uk for example) and then click on the options to design your own website. It is very simple and you don't need computer skills to do this – honestly! You can even upgrade to options that include your own checkout facility, which is great if you are selling online. The service also includes full email packages.

Telephone

Don't spend money on a second line for business. There are other ways to avoid giving out your home phone number. If you have broadband, your service provider may offer a hub phone or internet phone line. Alternatively, you could purchase a free sim card on a pay as you go scheme to use for receiving business calls. If you have broadband you can opt for a VoIP service, such as Skype. You can purchase telephones that connect to your hub or computer. If friends and family join Skype you can talk to each other for free.

Business cards

You can buy personalised business cards for under £10. Keep them simple and make sure they tell the reader everything they need to know. I like Moo (www.moo.com) and Vista (www.vistaprint.co.uk).

Staff

Can't afford staff but would like some help with the admin and answering the phone? Why not employ the services of a virtual office. I have used Moneypenny and they are fantastic, but there are many others to choose from, with monthly outlays a fraction of the cost of employing staff.

On the move

Working away from your office can be a nightmare when you need to access important bits of data. The problem is solved with logmein (www.logmein.com). You can now access your home or office computer from anywhere in the world – and, best of all, it is free to use!

Working with food

If you are preparing food, you may need a licence and approval. For more information contact the food standards agency on www.food.gov.uk or 0845 606 0667.

Start-up funds

Need some money to start your business? Depending on where you live, you may be eligible for help. Contact Business Link on 0845 600 9006 for help and advice.

Retraining

Maybe you would like to retrain in a new career. There are some great courses available both part-time and full-time. If you are concerned about cost, you may be eligible for a Career Development Loan – available for courses up to £8,000 (see www.lifelonglearning.co.uk or phone 0800 585 505). When I trained as a nutritionist, I worked from home with a personal tutor and attended university courses on a part-time basis, enabling me to work and study at the same time.

The Open University has developed a free resource designed to help educate people out of the recession. www.open.ac.uk/recession gives access to free educational resources, top tips for getting jobs and advice about accessing financial assistance for fee-charging courses. There are many government initiatives to help you retrain. Visit Directgov at www.direct.gov.uk and click on Education and Learning.

You're Hired!

Thinking about a new career? Speak to your local employment agencies to see what could tempt you. If you are looking for a part-time opportunity, you may like to become your own boss and salesperson. www.familyfriendlyworking.co.uk has a huge list of ideas. Here are a few I have put together.

- Utility Warehouse, a provider of cheaper utility prices, offer money-earning opportunities to those who would like to help spread the word about their service. You could become part of their team and earn commission on the usage of everyone you recommend for as long as that person is a customer – which means you will still be paid even if you leave. There is a great video online showing more information at www.utilitywarehouse.biz

- The Body Shop at Home. Earn money on selling body shop products to your friends and family or start a local party scheme. Call 0800 0929 090.

- Avon Calling. Avon has had a revival since the recession began. To sign up, visit www.avon.uk.com

- Herbalife is a global nutrition and direct selling company that has over 1.9 million distributors in over 70 countries across the globe. For more information visit www.herbalifeww.com/uk

- Kleeneze are one of the UK's longest standing direct selling companies with a heritage dating back 85 years. To find out more about distribution go to www.kleeneze.co.uk

- Fancy selling cosmetics and skincare products? Why not become a distributor for www.oriflame.co.uk, www.virginvieathome.com, www.marykay.co.uk or www.globalsales.myarbonne.co.uk

- Spreadshirt allows you to create your own designer t-shirts and other clothing on the website and open your own online 'shop' without any start-up costs or overheads. It is good for earning extra cash or for fund raising for schools and clubs with themed t-shirts etc. Visit www.spreadshirt.net

- Opinium Research (www.opinium.co.uk) pays people for their thoughts and opinions. In exchange for people's time responding to a survey they pay an average of 50p per survey.

- My Secret Kitchen (www.mysecretkitchen.co.uk) is the UK's first nationwide food and drink tasting company. They seek consultants to host parties, showing a range of lovely food and ingredients with recipe ideas to go along with them.

Money for Old Rope

You can earn money from your home – it may be from the spare room or unwanted items. Here are some ideas:

- If you are a homeowner, you could rent out your spare room. You can earn up to £4,000 a year tax free. See www.upad.co.uk for information and fact sheets.
- Do you have a beautiful home or classic car? You could register for your home or car to appear in films or TV – see www.mylocations.co.uk Or maybe you would love to be a film extra – see www.filmextras.co.uk
- If you live in a city, why not rent out your parking space or garage – see www.parklet.co.uk
- Become a house sitter, pet sitter or even a dog walker. You don't need any special equipment or skills – though an honest nature and love of animals would be pretty essential!
- EBay is the leading auction site for a reason. It is popular and if you follow the right procedures, it is safe. Simply photograph your item and list it as honestly as possible. Add your postage costs (use

Royal Mail pricing as a guide) and away you go. When sending sold goods, always get proof of postage. PayPal is the safest way to accept and receive payments. If you are not very technical www.stuffusell.co.uk and www.trading4u.com will do all the work for you, so sit back and take the money.

- www.musicmagpie.com is a great site to sell your unwanted music, DVDs and games.
- www.amazon.co.uk is another of my favourite websites for selling unwanted items but they do charge more in fees than eBay. However there is no listing fee so you only pay if your item sells.
- Why not hold your own boot sale? One person's junk is another's treasure. Bring plenty of change, carrier bags and food to keep you going. Any left over items can be given to a charity shop or put on Freecycle (www.freecycle.org).
- Cash Generator stores throughout the UK offer money for unwanted items and you can buy discounted used goods. This is great for a quick money fix but you are less likely to get the full price from these kinds of dealers, as they need to include their own mark up before selling on.
- Alamy (www.alamy.com) can help both seasoned professional and enthusiastic amateur photographers earn extra money. Anyone with a good quality digital camera and an eye for a good snap can sign up and generate income from their photos. Some contributors earn thousands of pounds a year through the site, many using their hobby to supplement the income from their day job.

Cash-back Sites

Now you really can earn money by doing very little. Cash-back sites are very simple. They link you through to day-to-day sites and you get cash back for every company link you purchase from. For example, if you are going to buy your shopping from Tesco.com you could visit www.quidco.com, register, link through, and you will receive cash back on your purchases. The best cash-back sites are:

- www.quidco.com
- www.topcashback.co.uk
- www.cashbackkings.co.uk
- www.ecashback.co.uk
- www.giveortake.com
- www.wepromiseto.co.uk
- www.rpoints.com
- www.freefivers.co.uk

Earn cash from your old mobiles

If you have an old mobile lurking in the back of a cupboard, get it out now and sell it online. Try these sites for cash-back deals for your old mobile:

- www.envirofone.com
- www.moneysupermarket.love2recycle.com
- www.mopay.co.uk
- www.mobilephoneexchange.co.uk
- www.mazumamobile.com
- www.bananagreen.com

Index

0870 numbers 27

activity holidays 162, 183–4
air travel 179

babyhood 147–54
baths and sinks 23, 25, 51, 54
benefits 7, 12
bins 49
blood 53
bogofs 74–5, 78
boilers 14, 20
bread maker 64
breakdown recovery 171, 176
broadband 26, 27, 30, 31, 166, 200
budget clothing 137–140
    holidays 180–7
    make-up 119–20
buying and selling your home 32–5

camping and caravanning 184–5
car rental 176–7
carpet freshener 58
cars 169–77
cash-back sites 206
CDs 159–60, 205
cinema 159–60
classic cars 171
clothing-swap parties 140–1
Co-op schemes 79

days out 153–4, 161, 162
designer for less 142–3
designer glasses 145
directory enquiries 28

dishwashers 18, 23, 47–8
disinfectants 43, 47
downshifting 42, 76
draught excluders 13
drains 49
driving lessons 166–7
DVDs 15, 142, 159–60, 194, 205

earning extra money 196–206
eco-breaks 137
electricity 9–20
    monitors 9–10
    switch 11–12
    tariffs 11
ethical clothing 138–40
exercise 151, 160–1

farmers' markets 79
fish dishes 98–100
freecycle 36, 64, 139, 150, 155, 161, 205
fridges and freezers 16, 17, 25, 48, 65, 66, 68, 72, 73
fuel costs 21, 22, 33, 173–5
furniture paste 52

games consoles 158, 159, 164
gardening 80–1
gas 9–20
gel air freshener 60
grow your own 80–1

hair dye 54
heating 20
hiring fashion 145
hob cleaner 46–7
hobby holidays 184

holiday swaps 181–3
home brewing 81
hostels 184

insulation 12–14
insurance 171–3

jam making 81–2

kettles 18–19

landfill 138–40
leather 56
library 160
lighting 16
loyalty cards 76

make do and mend 188–95
make your own gifts 193–5
massage 121–5
meat dishes 94–7
menstruation 135
mildew 51
mineral make-up 119
mobile phones 29–32
museums 160
music downloads 165–6
musical instruments 155

National Trust 152
natural skincare recipes 125–34

oven cleaner 46

pets 59
prepaid credit cards 165

rail transport 177–8
recipes 85–115

red wine 54
retraining 202

sales representative 202–4
scented candles 57–8
secondary double glazing 12
showers 23
slow cooker 64
social networking 155–7
spa 121–5
spilt milk 55
spot busters 134, 135
stains 53–6
standby 15
steamers 16
surface cleaner 47

tax 175–6
teenagers 163–7
telephone 26–9
telephoning overseas 28
toddlers 147–54
toilets 23–4, 49–50

utility bills 9–0

vegetarian 100–15
vintage clothing 143

wall marks 54–5
washing machines 17–18
water bills 23–6
weekend breaks 186
windows and mirrors 50–1
wood and laminate 52
working holiays 183–4